Negotiating To Settlement In Divorce

Negotiating To Settlement In Divorce

Sanford N. Katz
Editor

Contributors:
Martin L. Aronson
Roberta F. Benjamin
Harry M. Fain
James T. Friedman
Edward M. Ginsburg
H. Joseph Gitlin
Wilbur C. Leatherberry
Carol B. Liebman
W. Patrick Phear
David S. Rosettenstein
Gary N. Skoloff

PRENTICE HALL LAW & BUSINESS

Copyright © 1987 by Prentice Hall Law & Business.
All rights reserved. No part of this publication may be
reproduced or transmitted in any form or by any means,
electronic or mechanical, including photocopy, recording, or
any information storage and retrieval system, without
permission in writing from the publisher.

Requests for permission to make copies of any part of the
work should be mailed to:

Permissions, Prentice Hall Law & Business
855 Valley Road, Clifton, NJ 07013

Printed in the United States of America

Library of Congress Cataloging-in-Publication Data

Negotiating to settlement in divorce.

   Includes bibliographical references.
   1. Divorce settlements—United States.   2. Equitable
distribution of marital property—United States.
3. Custody of children—United States.   4. Negotiation.
I. Katz, Sanford N., 1933–   .   II. Aronson, Martin L.
KF535.Z9N44   1987   346.7301'66   87-14530
                                 347.306166
ISBN   013-610932-2

*To
Melba S. McGrath*

CONTENTS

Acknowledgments ix
Contributors xi

                    Introduction   xiii
                    Sanford N. Katz

CHAPTER ONE   A Theoretical Basis for
                    Divorce Negotiation   1
                    — Carol. B. Liebman —

The Changing American Family 1
Theories about Negotiation 4
   The Fisher and Ury Rules 6
   The People and the Problem 8
   Interests, Not Positions 9
   Generate Options 10
   Objective Standards 11
   The Best Alternative 11
   Two Negotiating Styles 13
   Rating Effectiveness 15
Characteristics of Divorce Disputes 16
The Risks of Adversarial Negotiation 19
The Negotiator as Role Model 21
Conclusion 24

CHAPTER TWO   Preparing the Client for
                    Successful Negotiation,
                    Mediation and Litigation   25
                    Wilbur C. Leatherberry

CHAPTER THREE — The Art and Craft of Successful Divorce Negotiation — 37
_ Gary N. Skoloff _

Principles of Negotiation 37
   Know Your Client and Your Client's Objectives.........37
   The Need for Complete Disclosure 38
   Be an Effective Communicator 38
   Developing a Strategy 39
Preparations for Negotiation 39
   Where Should the Negotiations Take Place?............40
   Should the Client be Present? 40
   The Timing of Negotiations 41
   Creating the Right Ambiance 42
Strategies 42
   Passive vs. Aggressive Behavior 42
   Gamesmanship: How to Offer, How to Bargain 42
   Emotions and Threats...............................43
   Interpreting Reactions 44
   Dealing with Deadlocks.............................44
Negotiation Ethics 45
   Lying and Manipulation 45
   Authority Issues 45
   Errors & Omissions 45

CHAPTER FOUR — The Four-Way Negotiation Conference — 47
_ Roberta F. Benjamin _

Why a Four-Way Conference? 48
When Not to Use Four-Way Negotiation 49
When to Hold a Negotiation Conference.................49
Where to Hold the Conference 51
How Many Conferences?..............................52
Preparation for the Four-Way Conference 52
Negotiation Style and Dynamics 53
   Style 53
   Dynamics 56

CONTENTS

Separate the People from the Problem 57
Focus on Interests, Not Positions 58
Inventing Options for Mutual Gain 59

| CHAPTER FIVE | Negotiating a Prenuptial Agreement
___ Harry M. Fain ___ | 61 |

Why a Prenuptial Agreement 62
Conditions for Prenuptial Agreements 63
Suggested Methods of Negotiating 64
Waiver of Support: Enforceability 66
Conclusion 69

| CHAPTER SIX | The Settlement Process—
the View From the Bench
_ Edward M. Ginsburg _ | 71 |

| CHAPTER SEVEN | Negotiating Under the
Demand of the Judge
_ Martin L. Aronson _ | 81 |

| CHAPTER EIGHT | The Dynamics of Mediation
___ W. Patrick Phear ___ | 89 |

| CHAPTER NINE | Negotiating Settlements of
Property, Alimony and
Child Support
___ H. Joseph Gitlin ___ | 111 |

The Five Stages of a Divorce Case 112
The Typical Facts: A Hypothetical 112
Fairness and Consistency: The Benchmarks of Good
    Settlements 113
Step One: Determine Percentage Distribution of Property .. 114
  Statutory Justification for Division of Property 115
  Tax Consequences of Property Distribution 115
  Property in Lieu of Support and Alimony 116

Who Gets What and Why 116
   Income-Producing Assets 117
   The Pension Plan 117
   Possession of the Residence 117
   Dividing Sale Proceeds of the Residence—Delayed Sale ... 118
   "Immediate" Sale of Residence 119
   The Pension Plan is Marital Property 122
   The Value of the Pension Plan 122
   The "If and When" Disposition of a Pension Plan 123
   Trading Off the Pension Plan 124
   Difficulties in Evaluating an Interest in Closely Held
      Corporation or Professional Practice 124
   Are Elements of a Professional Practice Income
      or Property? 125
   Individual Retirement Accounts 126
   Distribution of Tax Shelters 126
Alimony 127
   Income-Producing Property 127
   Wife's Employment Income 128
   Effect of Being Custodian of Children 128
   Tax Consequences of Alimony 128
   The Prospective Budgets of Each Party 129
   The Concept of Rehabilitative Alimony 130
Child Support 131
   Statutory Minimum Child Support Guidelines 131
   The Dual-Income Family and the Guidelines 132
Conclusion 132

CHAPTER TEN   **Negotiating Child Custody**
                          Cases   **133**
                          — James T. Friedman —

Positioning the Client for Negotiation or Trial 134
Timing of the Negotiation 136
Alternatives to Trial as Factors in Negotiation 137
Joint Custody 138
Leverage 139
Negotiating Techniques 142
Conclusion 142

CONTENTS

CHAPTER ELEVEN   A Divorce Negotiation
Problem: Developing a
Strategic Approach   **143**
David S. Rosettenstein

The Problem 146
Developing an Approach 151
   Introduction 151
   Know the Law 153
   Know the Facts 155
   Negotiating Policy and Ethics 157
   Preparing for the Negotiation..................... 159
   Negotiate 162
   Post-Negotiation Analysis.......................... 162
   A Possible Timetable for Use In a Seminar Course 165
Annexure A
   Confidential Instructions to Tom's Attorney 166
Annexure B
   Confidential Instructions to Mary's Attorney 168

Index **171**

Acknowledgments

The idea for a book on negotiation in family law matters was first suggested to me by Lynn and Steve Glasser, my publishers, who saw a need to educate the matrimonial bar in humanizing the divorce process by minimizing court appearances. The Glassers helped me to organize two conferences for lawyers, one in New York City and another in San Francisco, to discuss the whole range of issues in divorce negotiation—from theory to practice. I am grateful to the lawyers who participated in both conferences, to the contributors to this book for their patience and cooperation, and to the Glassers for their encouragement and support.

I wish to thank Dean Daniel R. Coquillette of Boston College Law School for his cooperation by making available to me the support services of Boston College Law School. In addition, I appreciate the technical assistance provided by Michael A. Perrino, a second-year law student at Boston College Law School, and Ms. Frances Piscatelli and the staff of the Word Processing Center at Boston College Law School.

I am especially grateful to Melba S. McGrath, my assistant, who, for a decade and a half, has given me wise counsel and perceptive editorial guidance. I know of no other person who loves language and respects "the word" more than she. I have thanked her privately in the past. On the occasion of the publication of this book, which coincides with her retirement, I wish to thank her publicly. It is to her that this book is dedicated—with admiration and affection.

Sanford N. Katz

Waban, Massachusetts
April 7, 1987

Contributors

Martin L. Aronson is a member of the Board of Governors of the Academy of Trial Lawyers. In addition to practicing law in Boston, Mr. Aronson teaches Negotiation and Evidence at Boston College Law School.

Roberta F. Benjamin practices law in Cambridge, Mass. She chairs the Family Law Committee of the Boston Bar Association.

Harry M. Fain practices law in Beverly Hills, Calif. He has served as chairman of the Section of Family Law of the American Bar Association and president of the American Academy of Matrimonial Lawyers.

James T. Friedman, a fellow of the American Academy of Matrimonial Lawyers, practices law in Chicago. He is the author of *The Divorce Handbook* (1982).

Edward M. Ginsburg practiced law in Boston before being named a judge of the Family and Probate Court in Cambridge, Mass. Judge Ginsburg teaches Family Law Practice at Boston College Law School and Suffolk University Law School.

H. Joseph Gitlin practices law in Woodstock, Illinois. A former chairman of the Illinois State Bar Association Family Law Section, Mr. Gitlin is a fellow of the American Academy of Matrimonial Lawyers.

Wilbur C. Leatherberry practiced with the Legal Aid Society of Cleveland, Ohio before joining the faculty at Case Western Reserve University School of Law. Professor Leatherberry organized and continues to supervise a course called Lawyering Process in which the instructors use simulation exercises to teach interviewing, counseling, and negotiating.

Carol B. Liebman practiced law in Boston before joining the faculty at Boston College Law School where she is the faculty director of the Boston College Legal Assistance Bureau. Professor Liebman also teaches a course on Mediation and has served as a mediator for the past five years.

W. Patrick Phear is a family mediator and is the director of Family Mediation Association, Inc., in Boston. Mr. Phear is a member of the Society of Professionals in Dispute Resolution, a director of the Association of Family and Conciliation Courts, and in the past served as the chairman of the American Arbitration Association's National Committee on Family Mediation.

David S. Rosettenstein is on the faculty of the University of Bridgeport School of Law. Professor Rosettenstein teaches courses in Family Law and Labor Law.

Gary N. Skoloff, a fellow of the American Academy of Matrimonial Lawyers, practices law in Newark, N.J., as well as being a member of the part-time faculty at Rutgers Law School, where he teaches Family Law. Mr. Skoloff has chaired the Family Law Section of the New Jersey State Bar Association and served as the editor-in-chief of the *Family Advocate*.

Introduction
Sanford N. Katz

Family law cases today constitute a great majority of the civil cases filed in American courts. If each of these filed cases were to proceed in normal channels of hearing and disposition (discovery of facts, hearing for temporary orders, further discovery, pretrial hearing, trial, and appeal), there is no doubt that our court system would be strangled. In light of this threat to the system, there is pressure on lawyers to negotiate a settlement.

There are decided advantages to a negotiated settlement. To begin with, a successful negotiation will result in far less court time, easing court burdens and placing less financial stress on the divorcing couple. Moreover by avoiding court confrontation, negotiation reduces the couple's psychological trauma and greatly increases the probability that they will comply with the final settlement. Indeed, divorce agreements reached by negotiation result in far fewer return engagements with the courts. Negotiation accords with the American spirit of independence and privacy, and with our dislike of bureaucratic bullying. In addition, successful negotiation helps the couple to understand that, although they are divorced and may even be remarried, their own relationship might continue for years to come, especially where children are involved. Finally, a successful negotiation teaches the couple techniques for resolving future disputes with each other without resorting to third-party assistance.

Yet the process of negotiation may simply be inappropriate for some couples or may have to be terminated abruptly without success. For example, if a client demands only vindication and victory or is temperamentally incapable of making a decision, or if the other spouse is persistently unreasonable, quarrelsome, or rigidly uncompromising, or if one spouse wants to change public policy, negotiation will not work. In such circumstances, it should not even be attempted or should be discontinued because it tends to result in inextricable gridlock, further emotional damage, and unproductive expense.

When negotiation is chosen, the negotiator operates within his or her own style, which can be adversarial or cooperative. Many lawyers tend to have adversarial negotiating styles and many social scientists tend to have cooperative styles. Of course, adversarial negotiators often cross over to cooperative methods when such methods may offer a better means of victory for their clients.

THE THEORY OF NEGOTIATION

Until recently, expert negotiation was considered an art, a kind of inborn talent that some people mysteriously possessed and others lacked; but the proliferation of books dealing with negotiation, both scholarly and popular, indicates that the rules and techniques of negotiation can be learned and successfully applied.

Unfortunately, the most publicized and imitated tactics have been the adversarial ones. In Professor Carol Liebman's striking phrase, the "barracudas" of the profession, those who treat each divorce controversy as a zero-sum game, have been the most visible.

There is, however, a growing body of works that offer proof of the greater and more lasting success of a cooperative approach to the resolution of divorce problems. Professor Liebman discusses and skillfully analyzes two current and influential works: Fisher and Ury's *Getting to Yes: Negotiation Agreement Without Giving In,* and Williams' *Legal Negotiation and Settlement.* She believes that the negotiating lawyer must choose his or her goals at her first meeting with opposing counsel. She is convinced that cooperative negotiation has a better chance of arriving at an agreement that will be effective in both the short and long term.

PREPARING THE CLIENT FOR NEGOTIATION

Professor Leatherberry stresses the vital importance of a sound relationship between attorney and client in divorce disputes, and the interviewing techniques that will produce it. The client must be able to speak freely, and must be secure in his lawyer's loyalty. By the same token, the lawyer must understand the client's needs, and have the tact and influence to guide the client into a reasonable settlement. Establishing this sound relationship should be the goal of the first meeting with the client.

Professor Leatherberry's article then points out the necessary requirements for successful advocacy on behalf of a divorce client. Probably the most important is the ability to listen well. "Listening well" does not mean being silent except when asking for an occasional clarification, nor does it mean that the client should be allowed to ramble unproductively. Inexperienced lawyers are often passive listeners, and rather than trying for a human relationship with the client, they take copious notes of everything the client says. The better approach is to become an active listener. An active listener will reword some of the client's details in a way that shows a full understanding and will occasionally venture beyond the client's direct presentation to ask questions suggested by the client's half-expressed emotions. Indeed, rather than shying away, lawyers should encourage clients to express their emotions during the interview and should take great care not to be judgmental.

Other important suggestions in this article are that the

lawyers must realize that final decisions rest with the client and that the lawyer must contract with, rather than trying to control, the client. The advocate should help to turn the client away from the past and toward the future, and should be able to recognize the stages that the client and the other party have reached in their dealings—stages uncannily like those of a terminally ill patient (denial, anger, depression, and finally acceptance). Of course, when the other spouse or opposing counsel is completely intractable, it may be necessary to call for the assistance of a judge, mediator, or referee to deal with the opposition directly.

NUTS AND BOLTS

Gary Skoloff is a seasoned attorney and his article reflects the adversarial inclination of lawyers in the field who focus on the big win. Even here, however all is not zero-sum. One of the important roles Mr. Skoloff assigns his negotiating lawyer is that of educating the client to understand the applicable laws and the procedures that take place in divorce litigation. When third parties (parents, friends, etc.) are involved in the affairs of the divorcing couple, they too should be made aware of the legal limitations and possibilities.

Mr. Skoloff's advocate must be in possession of every fact, especially facts relating to the parties' finances, since adversarial lawyers too often resort to manipulation and concealment to gain advantages for their clients. Moreover, the lawyer must learn to understand not only verbal communication but subtler nonverbal gestures—a movement of the eyes, a stiffening of the jaw, a slight tremor of the hand. If his client is unable to control such giveaways, it may even be better to stop bringing him or her to negotiating sessions.

Once the lawyer is certain of all the facts, it is important to develop a full strategy, flexible but basically dependent on the client's goals, or at least consistent with them. Some of the other topics discussed in this piece are the timing, locale and ambience of the negotiating sessions, the presence or absence of the client, the advantages and disadvantages of aggressiveness, and the uses of "gamesmanship." The discussion of ethics for the adversarial lawyer points out the fine line between exaggeration and fraud in negotiating, and stresses the importance of never exceeding one's authority and of remaining the agent of the client.

Although Mr. Skoloff veers strongly toward adversarial techniques, in the areas of custody and visitation, he reverses his approach, pointing out that such methods can lead to disaster for both parents and above all for the children.

FOUR-WAY NEGOTIATION

Roberta Benjamin describes the four-way conference (which involves both parties and their lawyers) as an ideal forum for solving legal problems in a divorce case. While such a conference retains an adversarial element, that element is somewhat muted. The actual physical participation of the couple gives them a sense of control and direct involvement in the solutions. What we have in such conferences is four persons acting to restructure the lives of two. It provides all of the participants with information and perceptions about the unique personalities and needs of the divorcing spouses, and should lead to tailor-made resolutions.

Benjamin argues that the ideal timing of a four-way conference depends on the particular emotional stage the divorce process has reached. She divides the divorce process into four emotional stages. "Holding on", the first stage, is characterized by a refusal to accept any responsibility for problems in marriage, resistance to physical change, rubbing the sore past like an aching tooth, depression, and a low energy level. The next stage involves a decrease in resistance, a better orientation toward the present, and a higher energy level. In the third stage, focus on the past diminishes and the party faces the present and the immediate future with increased energy. The final stage, "stabilization," usually occurs after the divorce. Attorneys find that the most effective timing for the four-way conference is between the third stage and the ultimate resolution. Because the spouses may arrive at different stages at different times, it is usually in both their interests to postpone the conference until both have reached a point when the attachment to the former spouse and lifestyle have loosened.

In this piece as in several others, the courthouse, with its almost hysterical pressures and interruptions, is not favored as the place to hold a negotiation conference; if at all possible, the conference should be held in the office of one of the attorneys. Nevertheless, Ms. Benjamin suggests that you may raise your opponent's hackles if your office is more elegant than his, causing him to become more aggressive. One or two conferences should suffice, and if one or both clients seem to want more, the attorneys should consider a cooling-off period. The negotiations are not meant and should not serve as group therapy. Preparation is the keynote for success. Options must be explored in the light of possible court action. This preparation involves more than "winning points." The clients must understand what claims, wishes and hopes can justifiably and legally be met and what ideas must simply be abandoned.

PRENUPTIAL AGREEMENTS

In Harry Fain's article we go, as it were, back to the future. Prenuptial agreements were once entered into almost exclusively by the very wealthy. Today, however, they have become increasingly popular, particularly between spouses who have previously married. It may seem exceedingly unromantic for two people contemplating the closest of human ties to contemplate at the same time the results, responsibilities and rights accruing to each if they should separate; but in fact, a careful prenuptial agreement may improve stability and harmony in marriage by clarifying and resolving issues before they become crises.

Parties enter prenuptial agreements for varying reasons, including their eagerness to avoid the trauma, emotional drain, and expense of divorce litigation; to protect separate property acquired before and during the marriage; to determine economic rights and obligations after the marriage; to protect a family business, a professional practice, or pension or retirement rights; to ensure fair treatment of children from former marriages; to provide maintenance or support provisions; and finally (though courts have not yet ruled uniformly on these issues) to contract for the religious upbringing of offspring.

The lawyer who negotiates a prenuptial agreement, like the divorce negotiator, must have a thorough knowledge of substantive law, the ability to discover the terms upon which the parties can agree, and the insight not to include terms the client does not intend to honor or provisions that the other party will find unacceptable. It is essential, moreover, to ensure that the agreement is ironclad with respect to any future attack based on fraud, misrepresentation, or coercion.

Finally the parties must be alerted to the risks inherent in any prenuptial agreement drafted today. Such agreements may be subject in the future to judicial modification or even become unenforceable if the couple's financial circumstances change dramatically over the years.

A JUDGE'S PERSPECTIVE

Judge Edward Ginsburg's article, "The Settlement Process—The View from the Bench," urges judges and lawyers in divorce cases to work together in order to change the public perception that the judicial system promotes conflict rather than fostering sound settlement.

Time is the first significant factor that the judge discusses. The busy lawyer may be tempted to postpone or continue matters which are less compelling to him than to the client, and some clients want to delay settlement as adverse to their interests, or in order to frustrate the other side. The judge begins by urging lawyers to be more sensitive to the impact of time—particularly delay—on the parties.

He then stresses a point that many contributors to this volume also emphasize: the setting of realistic expectations for both parties to the broken marriage. The client must face and learn to accept that the judicial system, at best, can only ensure a fair division of whatever funds are available and make the least harmful arrangements possible for the minor children of the marriage.

The reasons for out-of-court divorce negotiation, the judge points out are several: The outcome of a trial is risky and unpredictable; the divorcing couple will have an ongoing relationship particularly where children are involved; charge and countercharge in court would be detrimental, if not disastrous, for a child; and the parties who share in formulating their own agreement are far more likely to comply with its terms than those who are supposed simply to obey a court order.

The most effective means for the judge to bring the parties together for negotiation, according to Judge Ginsburg, is a uniformly enforced pretrial order requiring the exchange of all relevant information (particularly financial) and a meeting of the parties and counsel in person before preparation of the pretrial memorandum for the court conference. The meeting should never be a last-minute huddle in the court corridors; physical surroundings conducive to relaxation and rational argument are more important to a successful negotiated settlement than many busy lawyers recognize. The next step, the pretrial conference, should be fixed well in advance, and fixed firmly. At the conference, the presiding judge plays an important role. He or she can help control an unrealistic or stubborn client. A court's statement that a proposed settlement seems reasonable can often resolve the case; it can suggest cosmetic changes to make the terms agreeable to both sides; it can provide guidance in complicated cases of marital assets; it can make a recommendation based only on the relevant facts. When material facts are in dispute, the judge must be careful to condition his or her recommendation upon future evidence.

Finally, the court must recognize that there are parties who refuse settlement and use the negotiating process. The judge in situations of recalcitrance must set an imminent trial date. Once a settlement is reached at the pretrial conference, it should be put immediately into writing. By means of definite and careful pretrial procedures, lawyers and judges can work together to settle cases quickly and with a minimum of pain for the divorcing couple.

JUDICIAL PRESSURE FOR SETTLEMENT

An appropriate companion piece to Judge Ginsburg's is practitioner Martin Aronson's "Negotiating Under Demand of the Judge." Although the article states flatly that counsel should always be aware that he or she is engaged in an adversarial process, it plays down the use of war paint and suggests that professional cooperation with opposing counsel can pay off.

This piece is eminently practical, and its advice obviously flows from experience with a wide variety of clients and judges. Mr. Aronson emphasizes, for example, that thorough familiarity with all the facts is the *sine qua non* for helping the client and impressing the court; that a good lawyer is always prepared for trial, even while working through negotiation to make trial unnecessary; and the lawyer must communicate fully with the client before any negotiation session. Full communication means not only learning the client's viewpoint and wishes, but instructing the client in the applicable laws and—when operating under a judge's demands—outlining for the client the judge's personality and idiosyncracies.)

There is an interesting discussion here of a point made in the previous article: the need to put an agreement in writing at the earliest possible moment. Counsel must ensure that the client does not feel unduly pressured or confused by such rapid action.

Some judges use a technique that Mr. Aronson believes has its dangers: requiring a pretrial conference, and if no settlement is reached, then ordering the case to trial that same day. The apparent assumption is that settlement is more likely, but this contributor questions whether it will be a fair settlement. A variation occurs when the parties are kept in the courthouse awaiting trial, in the hope of their reaching agreement. The lawyer who believes the judge is bringing undue pressure must be tactful but firm, indicating a willingness to continue discussions but never abandoning the client's bottom-line position.

MEDIATION

The mediator, unlike the negotiator, cannot take the side of either party. The mediator is a trained neutral whose role is to help the parties themselves frame the resolutions that will be satisfactory to both.

The first duty of the mediator is to clarify the scope of the mediation. He or she must screen out issues that are basically psychological or fall into areas of substantive law; must secure formal agreements from both parties that they will act in good faith and will make full disclosure of all facts and relevant details; must explain the limits of confidentiality state; and must not offer advice to either party, although necessary substantive information can be provided. Both parties should use outside advisers whenever an issue requires partisan advice; any final agreement will be endorsed by a judge before it becomes binding.

Patrick Phear, in "The Dynamics of Mediation," outlines the perimeters of mediation and describes a hypothetical case, its successive stages, and its successful outcome. Courts consider the reaching of an agreement to be the measure of success, but community programs reach more deeply to ask how well an agreement meets the needs of the parties and how well it will withstand the pressures of time and changing circumstances. The mediator must serve as a kind of orchestra conductor who allows each side to present its theme and then skillfully leads the themes into common resolution, the mediator must be a semanticist who can reword complaints into acceptable viewpoints. He or she must always be in charge and yet allow both parties to feel that they are dealing with each other and not with the mediator. Without exerting pressure, the mediator must make the parties aware of financial restraints, the difficulties of new living arrangements, and the

INTRODUCTION

children's needs. And he or she must also indicate clearly that a mutually acceptable deadline must be set for termination of the process.

Special dangers face the lawyer-mediator, the most obvious of which is the prohibition of dual representation. But the lawyer-mediator who can walk the fine line of guiding without advising can help a divorcing couple make significant strides.

PROPERTY, ALIMONY, AND CHILD SUPPORT

Attorney H. Joseph Gitlin, writing on the negotiation of property, alimony, and child support issues in a divorce, also uses hypothetical cases to illustrate his points. He advises operating from as many strengths as can be devised—in other words, adversarially. Nevertheless, he points out that a lawyer insensitive to the other side's emotions and needs will weaken that lawyer's own position; the client must be convinced that the goal is a fair agreement and not victory per se. The first essential steps will be gathering all relevant facts, categorizing these facts, and evaluating financial data. Only after this will the lawyer move into actual negotiation and from there either to settlement or trial. The hallmarks of a successful negotiation are fairness and consistency. Striving for fairness and consistency is not only wise tactically but will enhance the lawyer's career by bringing the lawyer a reputation for being fair as well as able.

Mr. Gitlin believes that a thorough familiarity with the Uniform Marriage and Divorce Act, the statutory scheme under the act, and interpretive case law will pave the way for determination of all financial issues. While equitable distribution does not require a 50/50 division of marital property, that is a logical place to start; from there one can move to the factors that make a different distribution desirable and fair. A justification of disproportionate property division should at least start with the relevant statutes and the case law.

The article goes on to discuss a considerable number of pertinent factors, situations, and possibilities: the tax consequences of property distribution, tax shelters, property in lieu of support and alimony, income-producing assets, the cost of maintaining and repairing the family residence, mortgage payments, and proceeds of a sale of the home. The disposition of pension plans receives particularly thorough consideration. The thorny problem of interest in a closely held corporation is approached carefully, as is the much-debated issue of valuing a professional degree, license, and practice.

The latter portion of this piece discusses alimony and child support. Again, many varied scenarios are presented and the best denouments, from the viewpoint of one party or the other, are written in.

Along with most of his colleagues, this attorney stresses that lawyers with all the facts at their fingertips can create alternatives that will be more satisfactory to both parties than a court decision would be. A judge cannot have the thorough familiarity with the circumstances, emotions, psychologies, and temperaments of the clients that will make a negotiated settlement more viable and lasting than a judge's conclusions.

CHILD CUSTODY

James Friedman contributes a discussion of negotiation of child custody cases. In this area, the possibility of emotional pain for both the couple and their child is greater than in any other. A position on custody can serve as a way to punish a spouse or as leverage for property and support issues. One parent may concede custody to avoid harming the child in an emotional court battle. The child may choose the wrong parent for many reasons—brainwashing by a parent, being made to feel guilty, the "pleasant" atmosphere of an overly permissive parent.

The attorney has the ethical responsibility, if he or she believes the client's position is clearly harmful to the child, to try to persuade the client to change that position. If the client is obdurate, the attorney may even feel ethically compelled to withdraw from the case. The adversarial method should not be used at the expense of the child's best interests.

INTRODUCTION

Nevertheless, practitioner Friedman does suggest a considerable number of adversarial techniques: creating leverage by discovering priorities of the other spouse; demanding concessions for your own concessions; physical possession of the child as a key to winning; using the domestic violence statute to improve your client's position; in interstate cases, using the Uniform Child Custody Jurisdiction Act and the Parental Kidnapping Prevention Act as guidelines for your client and remedies against the opponent; and thwarting the other spouse's timing priorities to gain leverage for your case. This author, however, also brings up the use of language to change the attitude of the other spouse—for example, by rewording demands to save face.

There is no one best way to negotiate in a child custody case, because the child, the clients, and their advocates will act and interact. Mr. Friedman does suggest some firm guidelines, however. The negotiator must be consistently credible, must have come to a prior agreement with the client, must be able to control the client or use the inability to control the client as leverage, and must be sure that the opposing advocate also has full authority from the other spouse to negotiate a settlement. Above all, he must make sure that a win is the child's win.

TEACHING NEGOTIATION

The final article brings divorce negotiation into the classroom. Professor David Rosettenstein presents a hypothetical problem to be used ideally in a law school seminar course, although the problem can be condensed to be part of a long classroom discussion. Grades would be based, rather startlingly, not only on written analysis but on the net financial benefit (or detriment) each student obtained for his hypothetical client, relative to the results of other class participants. Professor Rosettenstein does tip his hat to the issue of child custody, which strictly speaking is outside the pale of monetary value, but leaves it to the student to develop his own personal viewpoint in that area.

This problem presents a scenario often appearing in divorce cases: the woman leaving school for marriage after high school; the man going shortly thereafter into law school; the birth of a son; the purchase of a home; the wife's continuing to work as a bank teller; and the husband's filing for divorce the day after he learns that he has passed the state bar examination. Both parties, in addition to divorce, are fighting over custody of their son, alimony, child support, property division under state law, and ancillary relief.

Details in this problem are meticulously described and include most of the issues appearing in divorce negotiations: the matrimonial home and furnishings, pensions, savings, cars, liabilities (such as car financing and student loans) and present and future employment of both parties. The financial information also deals with the expenses for the child, down to food costs, share of utilities, transportation, medical and dental bills, and even the effect on income tax.

The students are first alerted that any settlement must depend on the ability of the client to meet the financial arrangements. The particular difficulties in divorce of establishing a "Best Alternative to a Negotiated Agreement"; the vital importance of the advocate's knowledge of the law and of all the facts; the lawyer's ethical responsibilities, particularly in gray areas; the absolute necessity for the attorney to be completely prepared for all opposing demands: All these intricacies are presented with clarity and force.

The final section deals with an important learning tool—the postnegotiation analysis. Every aspect of the settlement would be separately discussed, including the style of the student negotiator and the effectiveness or failure of the agreement to protect the client.

This might well prove a valuable course in law schools. Many schools do have courses in negotiation, but few have focused in a credited seminar on the special techniques necessary for divorce negotiation.

CONCLUSION

Many temperaments and experiences have gone into the writing of these articles, and yet an overall image does emerge. All the contributors agree on the value of negotiation when it is viable, whether court-ordered or voluntary. All agree on the dangers and sometimes, for one party, the disasters—of courthouse agreements. The need for an advocate to have at his or her fingertips a complete and detailed knowledge of the facts, particularly the financial facts, and of all relevant laws and statutes is repeatedly stressed. And all underline the need for an attorney to be able to "read" his or her client (paying attention both to what the client says and to the client's unexpressed emotional reactions) and the absolute requirement that an attorney never exceed his or her authority in representing the client.

A split does occur in the basic philosophies attorneys bring to the negotiation process. The adversarial lawyer would seem to aim for a winner-take-all resolution favoring his or her client; the cooperative negotiatior believes that fairness is all. Yet even here there are crossovers. Most adversarials will pay at least lip-service to a fair settlement, and cooperatives, faced with overbearing tactics, may retaliate with a few ruses of their own, even the threat of withdrawal.

Not every lawyer in the gray area of child custody negotiation will consider the child's interests to be paramount. Perhaps this is the greatest danger for the out-and-out adversarial negotiator—winning custody of the child for the client even when the child might be better off with the other party. Of course, determining with whom a child will flourish best is far from simple, given the protestations of mother-love or father-love and the sometimes skewed wishes of the child. The truly ethical negotiator will make every effort to secure the best possible home for the hapless victim of divorce, and if need be will exercise his or her subtlest skills in persuading the client when that "best possible" conflicts with the client's expressed wishes and demands. It may be in this field that the cooperative negotiator will earn his or her greatest and truest triumphs.

CHAPTER ONE

A Theoretical Basis for Divorce Negotiation

Carol B. Liebman

THE CHANGING AMERICAN FAMILY

In the past 20 years, family law practice has changed enormously, becoming more complicated, more demanding, and more interesting. The changes in the work of the family lawyer reflect striking changes in the structure of the American family:

- The divorce rate has risen. It is estimated that almost half of all current marriages will end in divorce.[1]

- The percentage of adult women who work has increased from 17 percent in 1940 to 32 percent in 1960 to 48 percent in 1980.[2] The number of working mothers has increased dramatically, leading to changes in the allocation of parenting responsibility.

- Couples are having fewer children, having them later, or deciding not to have them at all.[3]

---

[1] L. Weitzman, THE DIVORCE REVOLUTION, xvii (1985).
[2] Weitzman, *Changing Families, Changing Laws*, FAM. ADVOC., Summer, 1982, at 2, 4.
[3] *Id.* at 4.

- More children live in families headed by a single parent. Close to 20 percent of all children under the age of 18 live in single-parent households.[4]

- Divorced individuals tend to remarry and to form new family units. An estimated 80 percent will remarry at some point in their lives[5], with a greater likelihood (at least for women) of remarriage if the divorce occurs before the age of 30.[6]

- Americans are more mobile. They no longer tend to live in the same community throughout their lives.

- Cohabitation without marriage is more common and more acceptable.

- Gay and lesbian relationships are increasing and are more openly acknowledged.

The traditional family of the 1960s—a breadwinner father and homemaker wife with two children—no longer dominates. Forty-five percent of American children will spend part of their lives in a single-parent household,[7] and a substantial portion of them will, at some time before the age of 18, acquire at least one stepparent.[8] The pattern evolving for many parents and children is movement through a series of expanding and contracting family relationships.

Changing family patterns both reflect and encourage changes in social values and attitudes. The impact of new behavior and new attitudes on family law has been profound:

---

[4] U.S. Bureau of the Census, *Marital Status and Living Arrangements: March, 1980*, in CURRENT POPULATION REPORTS 20 (No. 365, Oct., 1985).

[5] U.S. Bureau of the Census, *Divorce, Child Custody and Child Support*, in CURRENT POPULATION REPORTS 23 (No. 84, June, 1984).

[6] *Id.*

[7] *Id. at 3.*

[8] *Id.*

- No-fault divorce is available in every state except South Dakota.[9] In 14 states, irretrievable breakdown is now the only grounds for divorce.[10]
- The focus in custody determinations has shifted from parental fitness to the best interests of the children.
- The presumption that the mother would win custody, especially if the children were of tender years, has been abandoned. The trend is toward statutory recognition of, and in some instances preference for, joint custody.[11]
- Equitable distribution of property has replaced title-based systems for division of property.
- States have moved toward uniformity in laws concerning the family.[12]
- Family law has increasingly become the subject of federal legislation[13] and constitutional litigation.[14]
- Grandparents and other relatives are gaining the right to visitation.[15]

---

[9]Freed & Walker, *Family Law in the Fifty States: An Overview*, 18 FAM. L.Q. 369, 379 (1985).

[10]*Id.*

[11]*Id.* at 435. *But see* W. Weyrauch & S. Katz, AMERICAN FAMILY LAW IN TRANSITION 520–21 (1983) for a discussion of this trend.

[12]*See, e.g.*, UNIF. CHILD CUSTODY JURISDICTION ACT (1974); UNIF. MARITAL PROPERTY ACT (1983); UNIF. MARRIAGE AND DIVORCE ACT (1974); UNIF. PREMARITAL AGREEMENT ACT (1984).

[13]*See, e.g.*, UNIFORMED SERVICES FORMER SPOUSES' PROTECTION ACT, 10 U.S.C. sec. 1072 (1982); DOMESTIC RELATIONS TAX REFORM ACT OF 1984, 26 U.S.C. sec. 2 (Supp. III, 1985); RETIREMENT EQUITY ACT OF 1984, 26 U.S.C. sec. 72 (Supp. III, 1985); CHILD SUPPORT ENFORCEMENT AMENDMENTS OF 1984 (Supp. III, 1985); PARENTAL KIDNAPPING PREVENTION ACT OF 1980, 28 U.S.C. sec. 1738A (1982).

[14]*Developments in the Law—The Constitution and the Family*, 93 HARV. L. REV. 1156 (1980).

[15]See cases cited in Freed & Walker, *supra* n. 9, at 451–54.

- In calculating a spousal support award, the courts look to such factors as need, ability to pay, economic potential of both spouses, and nonmonetary contributions to the marriage rather than fault.
- Some courts have used implied contract theory as the basis for the award of support payments and division of property upon the dissolution of nonmarital heterosexual and homosexual relationships.[16]
- In a few instances, courts have imposed a support obligation on stepparents.[17]

All of these changes mean that standards for determining child custody and spousal maintenance have become more complex and sophisticated—and less predictable. With the growth of no-fault divorce, factual findings about behavior during the marriage are no longer available to guide the court in awarding custody or making support awards.

THEORIES ABOUT NEGOTIATION

Changes in families and consequent changes in the law naturally have had an impact on family law practice. There is more business, but the work is harder and more sophisticated, and requires greater skill. Since most divorce disputes continue to be settled before trial—fewer than 10 percent of all divorces actually go to trial[18]—the lawyering skill put to the greatest test is negotiation.

Negotiation is widely used, not only by lawyers but by businessmen, diplomats, parents, children, spouses, lovers, friends, and colleagues. Until recently, many discussions of negotiation treated it as an art—we knew that some people did

---

[16]*Id.* at 457–63.

[17]Foster & Freed, *The Obligation of Surrogate Parents: Where Does the Buck Stop?* 36 JUV. & FAM. CT. J. 97 (1985).

[18]Foster & Freed, *Joint Custody: Legislative Reform*, TRIAL, June, 1980, at 22.

NEGOTIATION THEORY 5

it very well, but we did not understand why. But in the past 15 years, a great deal of scholarly and popular literature has been devoted to negotiation. In fact, negotiation has become a growth industry. Unfortunately, high-risk, high-cost, adversarial negotiation techniques have been the most visible and most publicized, and have been too frequently emulated. Books on the bestseller list promise that readers can learn to out-negotiate any adversary, defeat any opponent. News stories glamorize the barracudas of the legal profession—the tough, break-them-or-take-them-to-court types who welcome the glare of publicity as they fight out their big-bucks cases. These lawyers measure their gains only in dollars and care little for the noneconomic impact of their negotiation tactics on the client, the other spouse, or the children. They view negotiation as just one more tool in the adversarial contest.

The adversarial approach to negotiation treats each divorce dispute as a zero-sum game. In a zero-sum game, every gain for one side means a loss for the other side. In effect, the negotiators are fighting over how to slice a pie, and a big slice for one client means less is left for the opponent. In a true zero-sum game, the size of the pie is fixed, and both parties value it equally. But there are few true zero-sum games. Even when it comes to slicing pies, one party may be willing to take a smaller piece of apple pie today, if he can be assured of getting a larger piece of chocolate pie next week.

In the last few years, works about negotiation have moved beyond analysis based on an adversarial view of negotiation to examine the actual behavior of lawyer-negotiators, or to set forth principles to guide negotiators. The result is a more sophisticated understanding of the types of behavior that contribute to effective negotiation.[19] This chapter will review two of those works: Fisher and Ury's *Getting to Yes*, which sets out

---

[19]To date there is no generally accepted standard for measuring the effectiveness of negotiation. Possible criteria include the economic value of the settlement, the impact on continuing relationships and fairness. On the subject of fairness, see Menkel-Meadow, *Toward Another View of Legal Negotiation: The Structure of Problem Solving*, 3 UCLA L. REV. 754 (1984).

principles for negotiators to follow, and Gerald Williams' *Legal Negotiation and Settlement*, which describes the differences in lawyers' negotiating styles. A lawyer who follows Fisher and Ury's recommendations and has the characteristics of the negotiator whom Williams labels an "effective cooperative" takes a problem-solving[20] rather than adversarial approach to negotiations.

Divorce disputes have special characteristics that make them especially appropriate candidates for problem-solving negotiations. After outlining those special characteristics, this chapter will discuss the pitfalls that await the adversarial divorce negotiator and, even more so, her client. Finally it will discuss a possible connection between lawyer conduct during negotiation and the client's ability to develop or improve his own conflict resolution techniques.

The Fisher and Ury Rules

Fisher and Ury, in the bestselling *Getting to Yes*, describe traditional negotiators as either hard or soft and find fault with both.[21] The soft negotiator so wants to avoid conflict that she gives up too much and, as a result, feels exploited. The hard negotiator views the negotiation as a contest with a winner and loser, and she battles for victory—even at the risk of driving the other side away from the negotiating table.[22] Fisher and Ury offer an alternative approach, which they call principled negotiation and which they encapsulate in four rules:

- Separate the people from the problem;
- Focus on interests, not positions;
- Generate a variety of possibilities before deciding what to do; and
- Insist that the result be based on some objective standard.[23]

---

[20]*Id.*
[21]R. Fisher & W. Ury, GETTING TO YES, xii (1981).
[22]*Id.*
[23]*Id.* at 11.

Although Fisher and Ury's principles may seem obvious and perhaps too aphoristic, they are often ignored by divorce lawyers who fail to see that divorce is not a zero-sum dispute. Let's examine how a lawyer who follows Fisher and Ury's method would negotiate a settlement in a hypothetical divorce dispute.

John and Susan have been married for eight years. They have one child, Tim, five years old. John earns $45,000 a year from his job as a salesman. Susan worked for five years as a social worker, including the first three years of the marriage, but gave up her job when Tim was born. She had been planning to look for a part-time job in the fall when he starts kindergarten. The family assets include equity of $16,000 in a house with an assessed value of $175,000. The initial downpayment of $12,000 was made with a gift of $6,500 from his family and $5,500 contributed by Susan from a small inheritance. While both parents are devoted to Tim, they have taken traditional roles in providing for his care. They have agreed that Tim should live with Susan, but John wants to be sure that he remains involved in Tim's life.

John's job has always required him to travel a great deal. When Susan was working, she did not mind his time away or his expectation that she would take care of the housework. Once Tim was born and Susan stopped working, she began to resent John's frequent trips and felt stuck at home. In the past few years, because of changes in employment patterns of the business world, an increasing number of John's customers are young females. Susan's resentment has turned into jealousy, and John feels that whenever he is at home, their conversations consist only of nagging and suspicious questions. Until recently John's relationships with his female customers were strictly of a business nature, but about six weeks ago he became involved with one customer and has been seeing her on a regular basis. Susan found out about the other woman and demanded that he move out of the house.

Fisher and Ury's principles apply with special force to divorce disputes between people such as Susan and John. Fisher and Ury contend that too often negotiators focus on the people involved in the dispute, arguing about who is to blame for the failure of the marriage without recognizing the emotional needs, values, and perspective of the other side.[24] The authors urge the negotiator to take the time to try to understand the dispute from the other party's perspective, to discuss differences in perspective, to avoid blaming the other side for the dispute,[25] to involve the other side in the process of developing a solution,[26] and to allow the other side to save face.[27] In their view, emotion plays an important role in negotiations. Negotiators should recognize their own and the other side's emotions, legitimizing these emotions by allowing them to be expressed without responding emotionally.[28]

The People and the Problem

Communication helps to separate the people from the problem. The negotiator is more likely to get the other side to listen to her arguments if she can show that she has heard her opponent, even when she disagrees with what the opponent has said.[29] Communication is enhanced by trying to avoid assigning blame, by understanding the other side's motivation, and by focusing on one's own perceptions rather than labeling, the other side's behavior.[30]

The problem facing Susan's and John's lawyers is to help their clients end the marriage and reconstitute the family into two units. If the lawyers assess blame for the failure of the marriage, or punish one spouse for real or imagined hurts, or try to satisfy their own ego needs—to win or to impress their clients by being tough—they are focusing on the people, not the problem, and as a result they escalate the conflict. In particular, arguing about who was to blame for the breakup of this marriage—John (because he failed to recognize Susan's

---

[24]*Id.* at 25–26.
[25]*Id.*
[26]*Id.* at 27.
[27]*Id.* at 29.
[28]*Id.* at 31.
[29]*Id.* at 35–36.
[30]*Id.* at 37.

feeling of isolation and became involved with another woman) or Susan (because her frustration at being trapped at home turned to jealousy, which kept her from appreciating John's effort to provide for her and Tim)—merely mimics the courts' backward-looking fault-finding and does nothing to solve the problem. Because the lawyers are involved in negotiation rather than litigation, they have the opportunity to help shape the future rather than label the past.

Interests, Not Positions

Fisher and Ury's second rule is to focus on interests, not positions. They point out that often it is easier to reconcile interests than positions because a particular interest usually can be satisfied in a number of ways.[31] Even when positions are incompatible, the underlying interests may not be.[32]

The lawyer who demands that her client get the house, and battles for the house no matter what the cost, is trapped into negotiation over positions, not interests. In all likelihood, Susan and John both will want the house. An exploration of the underlying interests by asking why each wants the house may open the door to a variety of solutions. Perhaps Susan wants to stay there to provide continuity for Tim, because of the quality of the neighborhood schools, or because neighbors will be available to babysit when she goes back to work. Maybe John wants the house as an investment because it is in a neighborhood where property values are expected to rise rapidly. Once these interests are identified, a way to structure an agreement satisfying the interests of both may emerge. For example, Susan stays in the house until Tim finishes school, then the house is sold, with John and Susan each receiving an agreed share of the proceeds. Similarly, if an attorney's goal is to ensure financial security for her client, the dependant spouse, she can investigate many options—lump sum payment, flow of income, support for education or job training—but these ave-

---

[31] *Id.* at 43.
[32] *Id.* at 43–44.

nues are foreclosed if the attorney gets stuck battling over a position.

Generate Options

Fisher and Ury's third rule is to generate options before deciding what to do. They urge negotiators to brainstorm and to come up with a range of options before reacting to the proposals. Negotiators, they say, should identify shared interests, look for opportunities for mutual gain, and explore the basis of separate interests.[33] The "Getting to Yes" view is that offers are more effective negotiating tools than threats. In contrast to adversarial literature or negotiation that discusses ways to make threats credible,[34] Fisher and Ury emphasize the importance of making offers credible.[35]

Lawyers who approach negotiations as an extension of the adversarial process can be blinded by competitiveness to the wide range of interests shared by the divorcing parties: interests in ending the dispute, reorganizing the family unit, protecting the children, and establishing both spouses on an independent footing financially and emotionally. These shared interests lend themselves to imaginative development of options if the negotiator is willing to take the time to listen to her own client and to the other side. In John and Susan's case, John's interest in being involved in Tim's life is consistent with what will no doubt be Susan's interest in having some time to herself free from the responsibilities of childcare, an interest that will grow when she reenters the work force. John's interest in limiting the length of time he must pay spousal support is consistent with Susan's desire to return to work.

---

[33]*Id.* at 73, 77.
[34]*See, e.g.*, G. Bellow & B. Moulton, THE LAWYERING PROCESS 548–61 (1979); H. Edwards & J. White, THE LAWYER AS NEGOTIATOR (1977).
[35]Fisher & Ury, *supra*, n. 21, at 82.

Objective Standards

Finally, Fisher and Ury urge that results be based on an objective standard. They identify three categories of objective standards: fairness, efficiency, and scientific merit[36] and point out that agreements conforming to common practice are likely to be the most acceptable.[37] Fisher and Ury suggest that the negotiator confronted with pressure tactics—threats, bribes, manipulative appeals to trust, refusal by the other side to alter a position—should respond by asking about the reason for the other side's position and by suggesting objective criteria to resolve the impasse.[38] Reference to objective standards, such as the use of a mutually acceptable appraiser to value the house or the business, is familiar to lawyers, although in the adversary context the process may deteriorate into a battle of experts.

Suppose that Susan's and John's negotiators, following the Fisher and Ury rules, developed satisfactory agreements about custody, visitation, support, and division of most of the assets, only to have the whole settlement threatened by an inability to agree on division of their personal property. This is a time for use of objective standards. The range of possibilities is wide. They could take turns picking items after flipping a coin to determine who picks first, or they could agree to divide property according to who brought the item to the marriage. Here, again, imagination and flexibility can contribute to effective dispute resolution.

The Best Alternative

In addition to offering their four rules, Fisher and Ury address the problem faced by a negotiator when the other side

---

[36]*Id.* at 86.

[37]*Id.* at 86. Fisher and Ury ignore the tension between their advice to be imaginative in generating options and their insight that the common solution is likely to be more acceptable to the other side.

[38]*Id.* at 94.

has more economic or emotional resources or a stronger legal position. They urge negotiators to know their Best Alternative to a Negotiated Agreement (BATNA), that is, to consider what their position will be if they do not reach a negotiated agreement.

The negotiator faced with a more powerful opponent should have two goals: avoiding reaching agreement if better options are available, and making the most of what she has.[39] They argue that by knowing the client's BATNA, a negotiator can avoid the dual hazards of giving up too much or being so tied to a notion of bottom line that the negotiator lacks the flexibility to be creative in working out an agreement.[40]

Traditional texts about adversarial negotiation teach that negotiators should always know their bottom line, the point beyond which they would rather litigate or lose the chance to make a deal, before beginning bargaining. Fisher and Ury agree that a negotiator should not enter discussions without an idea of the limits beyond which she will not be willing to reach an agreement. But they criticize the bottom line approach for two reasons. First, it inhibits the negotiator's ability to adjust a bargaining position in light of information received during the negotiation. Second, since most negotiators set their bottom line too high, they risk walking away from the bargaining table when the available terms meet more of the client's interests than any other available option (such as litigation or making the deal with someone else).[41]

Establishing a BATNA is easy if you are representing a baker in negotiations with a fruit wholesaler for the purchase of strawberries. You can check the prices with other wholesalers or estimate the cost of substituting a different fruit (considering both the purchase price and the baker's loss of sales to strawberry tart lovers). In the divorce context, it is less easy to determine a client's BATNA, and the alternatives are limited: litigate despite high economic and emotional costs and an uncertain outcome; put off the negotiation and the litigation,

---

[39]*Id.* at 101.
[40]*Id.* at 104.
[41]*Id.* at 103.

leaving the parties in a warlike state of hostility and uncertainty; or perhaps try mediation or new lawyers.

Two Negotiating Styles

The work of Gerald Williams[42] lends support to the proposition that adversarial negotiation is a risky way to resolve divorce disputes. Williams studied lawyers' behavior. He asked 600 lawyers to describe opposing counsel in their most recently completed case in terms of 137 characteristics and then to rate them as effective, average, or ineffective negotiators.

Williams points out that a lawyer's effectiveness can be measured not only by the economic benefit produced for the client but also by the social, psychological, and monetary costs of resolving the dispute, whether all issues are settled, the stability of the agreement, whether damages to both parties are minimized and benefits to both maximized, whether "applicable rules, customs, and etiquette" were observed, and whether the settlement process represented an "efficient use of available resources."[43] However, the lawyers in the study were not provided with criteria for measuring effectiveness, rather, they were left to apply a subjective standard.[44]

Williams' study identified two styles of lawyer-negotiators, cooperative and competitive. He found that 65 percent of the lawyers studied could be described as cooperative and 24 percent as competitive. Style was not necessarily an indicator of effectiveness; some cooperative negotiators were effective, as were some competitive negotiators.

Williams makes it clear that "cooperative effectives" and

---

[42]G. Williams, LEGAL NEGOTIATION AND SETTLEMENT 39 (1983). [hereinafter Williams, LEGAL NEGOTIATION]. G. Williams, LEGAL NEGOTIATION AND SETTLEMENT: A LAWYER'S HANDBOOK FOR EFFECTIVE NEGOTIATION AND SETTLEMENT (1984) [hereinafter Williams, HANDBOOK].

[43]Williams, LEGAL NEGOTIATION, *supra* n. 42, at 9.

[44]*See* Menkel-Meadows, *supra* n. 19, at 815 (discussion of whether fairness is a criterium that should be included in any evaluation of the effectiveness of a negotiated agreement).

"competitive effectives" approach negotiation with different mindsets. According to Williams, "cooperative effectives seek to facilitate agreement, they avoid the use of threats, they accurately estimate the value of cases they are working on, they are sensitive to the needs of their clients, and they are willing to share information with their opponent.... They are apparently as concerned with getting a settlement that is fair to both sides as they are with maximizing the outcome for their own client."[45] By contrast, effective competitives are concerned not only with maximizing the outcome for their client, but they appear to take a gamesmanship approach to negotiation, having a principal objective of outdoing or outmaneuvering their opponent. Thus rather than seeking an outcome that is 'fair' to both sides, they want to outdo the other side; to score a clear victory."[46] This is the adversarial, zero-sum approach to negotiation.

Nonetheless, the effective cooperative negotiator and the effective competitive negotiator have a number of characteristics in common. Both are seen to be experienced, ethical, trustworthy, honest, prepared in terms of the facts and the law, realistic, rational, analytical, astute about the value of their own and their opponent's case, skilled in picking up cues from the other side, perceptive about their opponent's strategy and their own reaction to that strategy. Both are considered effective trial attorneys and both follow the customs and courtesies of the bar.[47]

By contrast, the ineffective cooperatives and the ineffective competitives have nothing in common. The ineffective competitive shows many of the traits of the insecure bully. She is irritating, arrogant, headstrong, and makes unreasonable demands.[48] The ineffective cooperative is the type of person social scientists would describe as "other directed." Not only trustworthy but trustful, not only polite but obliging, she is intelligent, dignified, and self-controlled, but possibly most

---

[45] Williams, LEGAL NEGOTIATION, *supra* n. 42, at 22.
[46] *Id.* at 24.
[47] *Id.* at 27–29.
[48] *Id.* at 39.

important, she is unskilled in reading cues and puts a premium on maintaining good relations with opposing counsel.[49]

Rating Effectiveness

Significantly, it seems more difficult to be an effective negotiator using a competitive style. In the Williams study a significantly higher proportion of the cooperative attorneys were rated effective.[50] Sixty-five percent of the lawyers were rated cooperative; 24 percent were rated aggressive (11 percent fit no discernible pattern). Only 25 percent of the competitive attorneys were rated effective, compared with 59 percent of the cooperatives. Even more striking, one third of the competitive attorneys were rated ineffective, compared with only 3 percent of the cooperatives. "Based on these statistics," Williams concluded, "it appears that it is significantly more difficult to be an effective/aggressive negotiator [than] an effective cooperative."[51]

Williams suggests the reasons it is difficult to be an effective competitive. The competitive negotiator runs substantial risks because of the tension and distrust that a competitive negotiating style produces. True, the competitive negotiator may be effective against an unskilled cooperative negotiator, and she avoids the risk of giving up too much.[52] But she runs a great risk of misunderstanding, especially of thinking the parties are further apart than they actually are; she risks retaliation and total breakdown of the negotiation. In fact, Williams found that effective competitives were twice as likely to go to trial as were effective cooperatives.[53] In addition, negotiations conducted by a competitive negotiator tend to take longer (and therefore have higher economic and emotional costs); and produce both lower joint outcomes and lower

---

[49]*Id.* at 34–35.
[50]*Id.* at 19.
[51]Williams, HANDBOOK, *supra* n. 42, at 16.
[52]*Id.* at 31–32. Williams suggests that competitives may also be somewhat better in complex negotiations. *Id.* at 31.
[53]Williams, LEGAL NEGOTIATION, *supra* n. 42, at 51.

individual outcomes.[54] Finally, lawyers with reputations as competitive negotiators may provide the other side with an incentive to prepare more thoroughly for the negotiation.[55]

Williams' data suggests it is easier to be an effective cooperative negotiator because the approach promotes understanding, produces agreement more quickly, and often provides greater individual gain as well as generally producing greater joint gain. However, the cooperative attorney does face some risks, especially the risk of exploitation by a competitive opponent. Williams notes that cooperatives "will tolerate a surprising degree of exploitation before recognizing what is happening to them"[56]; they "are vulnerable to exploitation, and they are slow to recognize it when they are being exploited by a skillful opponent."[57] In addition, the cooperative risks overreacting to the unfairness of competitive tactics by escalating the conflict and, ultimately, letting negotiations break down.[58] Williams also notes that the ineffective cooperative, by making too many concessions, causes her opponent to increase expectations and become more demanding.[59]

Significantly for divorce negotiators, Williams points out that competitive negotiators are likely to damage long-term relationships that depend on mutual trust.[60]

CHARACTERISTICS OF DIVORCE DISPUTES

A divorce dispute has special characteristics that present opportunities for effective problem-solving if the lawyer has the mindset and skills of Williams' effective cooperative lawyer and follows Fisher and Ury's rules. Many of the same

---

[54] Williams, HANDBOOK, *supra* n. 42, at 31–33. Williams also notes that unprepared competitives do much worse. *Id.* at 33.
[55] *Id.*
[56] *Id.* at 36.
[57] *Id.*
[58] *Id.*
[59] *Id.*
[60] Williams, LEGAL NEGOTIATION, *supra* n. 42, at 52.

characteristics pose special dangers for the adversarial negotiator.

Among the special characteristics are the following:

- Divorce disputants have a long history and in most cases will continue to interact in the future. While the marriage is ending, the family continues. The parties are struggling to let go of the spousal relationship at the same time that they are working to restructure the family relationship.
- The dispute is highly emotional.
- The parties have a great deal of information about each other.[61]
- The range of solutions courts are empowered to impose are limited, crude, and unresponsive to individual needs.
- Enforcement of court-ordered resolutions is difficult.

The disputants' long history and the likelihood of future interaction mean that the parties have a number of common interests. Part of the lawyer's job is to help the client cut through the emotion, bitterness, and pain of the moment to recognize these shared interests, and to build an agreement that satisfies as many common interests as possible. The most important are concern for the children; the need to maximize available financial resources; the need to make the dependent spouse, usually the wife, self-sufficient; and the need to restructure the family relationship to allow the spouses and the children emotional peace.

In a divorce conflict, because of the intensity of the family relationship, the people tend to become the problem.[62] As a result, the parties may need their lawyers' help to focus on designing a new structure for the family. Without that help they will instead spend their time and energy replaying history

---

[61]Rubin, *Third Party Intervention in Family Conflict*, 1 NEGOTIATION J. 269, 270–71 (1985).

[62]*Id.* at 273–274.

and trying to place blame for the marital breakup. An adversarial lawyer will escalate the conflict by encouraging personal attacks and fault-finding.

While the nature of the family relationship may cause the disputants to experience greater emotional turmoil than in most other disputes, it also provides them with the potential to separate positions from interests.[63] The interdependence of family members means each divorce disputant has a great deal of information about the other's underlying interests and motives.[64] This information can make it easier for them to recognize and respond to the interests behind any negotiating position. The problem-solving lawyer can use the client's insights to respond to the interests behind the other spouse's position rather than arguing about positions that may be only symbolic of underlying interests.

Because court-imposed solutions are often crude and unresponsive to the disputants' needs and those of their families, and because it is difficult to predict court outcomes in divorce cases, the parties have strong incentives to work out their disagreements during negotiation.

Finally, the difficulty of enforcing court-imposed solutions to a divorce dispute gives parties a powerful incentive to reach an agreement that satisfies both, or at least seems fair to both. Parties are much more likely to comply with the terms of an agreement than with the terms of court-imposed order.

It is important to note that some disputes are not appropriate for negotiation.[65] Some divorces have to go to trial because the client needs a victory, not a settlement; because the client does not want responsibility for the decision; because the other side is unreasonable; or because one spouse wants to establish new legal norms. For example, a bitter and angry spouse may need a court judgment labeling the other spouse as at fault. If the marriage has included a history of abuse, the nonabusive spouse may be unable to take responsibility for

---

[63]*Id.* at 273.

[64]*Id.* at 270.

[65]*See* Menkel-Meadows *supra* n. 19, at 829. *See also* Williams, LEGAL NEGOTIATION, *supra* n. 42, at 10–12.

assenting to any continued contact between the abuser and other family members. If one side in a negotiation is behaving unfairly, using delay or high-pressure tactics to wear down the other side, litigation may be the only way to end the unreasonable behavior. For a father who 15 years ago sought custody of a young child, litigation may have been required to reorder public policy.

Although there are many reasons for turning to litigation, the overwhelming percentage of divorces will continue to be resolved through the negotiation process. The fact that more than 90 percent of all divorces are resolved through negotiation is a measure of the potential benefits of the negotiation process, but that statistic also masks the grave harm that occurs when negotiations become adversarial.

THE RISKS OF ADVERSARIAL NEGOTIATION

The lawyer who conducts negotiation as an adversarial contest, who comes to negotiation with the mind-set of Williams' competitive negotiator, who ignores Fisher and Ury's rules, and who treats the negotiation as a zero-sum game, is likely to miss opportunities to maximize gain for both spouses and to heighten their emotional conflict. Adversarial negotiation precludes the opportunity to generate options, the cornerstone of problem-solving negotiation. Instead, adversarial negotiation views bargaining as a series of concessions to be forced from the other side, while giving up as little as possible.

Adversarial divorce negotiation has a number of risks and costs. First is inappropriate linkage of issues. In its most common and most tragic form, inappropriate linkage ties time with the children to support for the wife. The wife's lawyer may threaten to limit the husband's time with the children unless he increases his support offer; the husband's lawyer may threaten to contest custody unless the wife lowers her monetary demands. Often these negotiating positions are contrary to both parties' instructions to seek a settlement that is best for the children.

What is the negotiator's responsibility in this situation? To do some reality testing—to help the client sort through priorities, to point out the inconsistency in wanting the best for the children while linking access to financial concessions. The lawyer who treats time with the children as something to be bargained away for monetary concessions almost certainly will increase the other side's levels of anger and mistrust and will cause the children and the parties needless pain and anxiety.

A second problem with adversarial negotiation is that it disempowers the clients. Initially one of the parties may be so shocked by the breakdown of the marriage that he wants to dump the whole problem on the lawyer's desk and let her handle it. As the divorce process develops, most clients will not only regain the ability to participate in the solution to the conflict, but in fact will feel ignored or pushed around by the lawyer if denied participation. Instructing a client not to talk to the other spouse, excluding clients from discussions about negotiation strategy, or ignoring a client's instructions increases a client's sense of loss of control over the dispute. The result is a frustrated, angry client in search of less alienating dispute resolution processes.[66]

Third, divorcing couples go through many emotional stages. The problem-solving negotiator can help the clients to let go of the marriage. A competitive negotiator, by contrast, often prolongs the process. Continued fighting may be a sign that a couple is having trouble letting go of the moribund marriage. If a lawyer doesn't recognize the psychodynamics of the fighting, if she focuses on the subject of the fight, not the process, she will at a minimum waste time and energy negotiating over issues that are not really important to the ultimate settlement. She may, by buying into the fighting, lose credibility with the other side's lawyer and, most serious, lose the chance to help the parties recognize what is happening. All too often she continues to fight over the substance even after the parties have moved on and are ready to make peace. The result is

---

[66] A staff member of one attorney disciplinary body informed the author that a high percentage of all complaints about attorneys involve divorce cases.

that clients needlessly continue fighting or, at the end of the divorce process, speak with contempt of their lawyers, blaming them for escalating and dragging out the conflict.

Fourth, because the adversarial negotiator views the negotiation as a win/lose competition, she misses the opportunity to generate options that let both parties win. For example, an adversarial negotiator who represents a father in discussions about visitation may demand overnight visits every weekend, meeting resistance to this demand with threats of reduced support or a custody fight. The wife and her attorney are put on the defensive, emotions escalate, and opportunities for expeditious and satisfying solutions to the problem are missed. In a problem-solving negotiation, the lawyers would identify their clients' interests: Does each of them want the children to have a good relationship with the other spouse? Is the husband worried that he will not be an important part of the children's lives? Does the mother want weekend time with the children because she plans to go back to work? Once the clients' interests are identified, the lawyers will see opportunities for a variety of visitation schedules that allow the father to be more than a weekend visitor and the mother to have child-free time during the week and relaxed weekend time with the children.

A fifth problem with adversarial negotiations is that the final agreement is likely to be unworkable. An agreement forced on one party through bullying, or an agreement accepted out of emotional or financial exhaustion, will feel unfair. It is likely to be broken; as a result, the parties will face continued conflict and repeated trips to court.

THE NEGOTIATOR AS ROLE MODEL

Lawyers teach their clients a great deal about how to dispute and how to negotiate. In social science terms, clients learn from observing behavior modeled by their attorneys. Even when the results of the negotiation appear successful, the lessons about dispute resolution often have been disastrous.

One of the parties' major tasks is to improve their dispute resolution skills. In fact, one cause of the divorce may well be the lack of these skills.[67] Former spouses will inevitably have differences after the divorce decree is entered. What the parties learn from their lawyers during the divorce negotiations may determine their success at restructuring the family and getting on with their separate lives.

Social learning theorists teach that "human behavior is transmitted, whether deliberately or inadvertently largely through exposure to social models."[68] Exposure to models may have one of three effects: the observer may learn new behavior; inhibition of previously learned behaviors may be strengthened or weakened, depending on whether the modeled behavior is rewarded or punished; or observation may help to bring previously learned responses to the fore.[69]

Attention seems to be the key factor in learning by observation. Learning from observation is enhanced when the modeled behavior is rewarded or when the model possesses certain positive characteristics.[70] The prestige, attractiveness, and power of the model have all been shown to increase the effectiveness of observational learning.[71] The existence of an affectional relationship between the model and the observer, the model's repetition of behavior, and the modeled behavior's success can also contribute to learning. In addition, an angry observer is more likely to imitate a model's aggressive behavior.[72]

Given what we know about modeling, it would appear that

---

[67] *See* S. Kessler, THE AMERICAN WAY OF DIVORCE: PRESCRIPTIONS FOR CHANGE (1975).

[68] Bandura, *Analysis of Modeling Processes*, in PSYCHOLOGICAL MODELING 1 (A. Bandura ed. 1971). *See also* Kahn & Cangemi, *Social Learning Theory: The Role of Imitation and Modeling in Learning Socially Desirable Behavior*, 100 EDUCATION 41 (1979) (summaries of articles and books dealing with social learning theory); Hosford, *Self-as-a-Model: A Cognition Social Learning Technique*, 9 THE COUNSELING PSYCHOLOGIST 45 (1980).

[69] Bandura, *Analysis of Modeling Processes*, supra n. 68, at 5–6.

[70] *Id.* at 13.

[71] Hosford, *Self-as-a-Model*, supra n. 68, at 47.

[72] *Id.* at 47–49.

lawyers are powerful role models for their clients. Lawyers are licensed by society to function as dispute resolvers. They have the expertise to guide disputants through the legal morass that surrounds a divorce. They serve as advocates at times when divorcing clients feel abandoned and vulnerable. Clients have frequent opportunities to observe their lawyers' negotiating behavior both in sessions preparing for negotiations between the lawyers and in four-way negotiations attended by parties and their counsel. And lawyers' appearance, their office surroundings and the demand for their time often seems to symbolize success.

Frequent attacks on the role of lawyers in divorce negotiation suggest that many attorneys lack adequate negotiating skills.[73] Few lawyers have been trained to be effective negotiators. Until recently, courses in negotiation practice or theory were rarely offered as part of the law school curriculum. In addition, many lawyer negotiators allow an adversarial approach to narrow their vision of the opportunities for conflict resolution during negotiation.[74]

The lawyer who links issues inappropriately reinforces this type of thinking by the client. The lawyer who plans for a negotiation session by thinking of ways to defeat the other side inevitably legitimizes this win/lose approach in the client's eyes. The lawyer who responds to offers with ad hominem attacks on the other lawyer or spouse encourages the client to place blame rather than explore options. The result in most cases is a client who has been taught to be an ineffective competitive negotiator, to view life as a zero-sum game, and to approach disputes determined to defeat the other side rather than looking for solutions that allow both to win.

---

[73]*See* Mnoonkin & Kornhauser, *Bargaining in the Shadow of the Law: The Case of Divorce*, 88 YALE L.J. 950, 986 n. 118 (1979). *See also* J. Haynes, DIVORCE MEDIATION 5–7 (1981).

[74]*See* D. Saposnak, MEDIATING CHILD CUSTODY DISPUTES 15–17 (1983) (critique of the adversary approach). *See also* Committee of the Family, Group for the Advancement of Psychiatry, NEW TRENDS IN CHILD CUSTODY DETERMINATIONS 67 (1980) (discussion of the problems for the child if the custody proceeding becomes adversarial).

CONCLUSION

Every divorce negotiator faces choices about her negotiation behavior—choices that the lawyer may be ethically bound to explain to the client. Choosing adversarial negotiation exposes the client to risks and costs that are particularly high in the divorce context. When a negotiator first meets with opposing counsel, she must make fundamental choices about her goals. Will she work for a settlement that feels fair to both spouses, or will she battle to win the most possible for her own client? The lawyer whose goal is a fair settlement will have a better chance at fashioning a workable agreement that will minimize future hostility. Of course, if she is ineffective, she risks getting too little for her client.

The lawyer who chooses to maximize client gain—to go for the win—risks increasing hostility to the point where the negotiation breaks down. She risks sowing, or at least fertilizing, the seeds of distrust and anger that will bear bitter fruit for years after the divorce decree is entered. This latter risk is one that few clients would choose.

CHAPTER TWO

Preparing the Client for Successful Negotiation, Mediation and Litigation

Wilbur C. Leatherberry

Both in practice and in clinical teaching, client interviewing is the most important and most overlooked lawyering skill. Because interviewing is so clearly an art rather than a science, we are tempted to assume that we do it well, or that improvement will come automatically with more experience, or that we will never be good at interviewing and counseling because of a basic lack of talent for the task. I am convinced that most lawyers do a poor job of interviewing and counseling and that all lawyers can improve their techniques by thoughtfully examining how they relate to clients.

Good interviewing and counseling techniques, important in any area of law practice, are especially critical in the domestic relations practice. Few divorce cases should go to trial. The financial and emotional litigation costs of the parties and their children are enormous. If a client's objectives must be achieved through a judicial decree, ill-feelings between the parties very likely will continue for a long time. One consequence is that noncompliance with at least some aspects of the decree is likely as well.

Interviewing and litigating require very different skills. An aggressive, adversarial posture, which the client may expect of his advocate in litigation is inappropriate in relations between lawyer and client. The matrimonial lawyer must be both an effective counselor and an effective advocate.

Sound interviewing techniques should produce a solid attorney-client relationship. The client will be able to discuss matters freely with the lawyer and will be confident of the lawyer's loyalty and understanding of the client's needs and objectives. If the case should have to be tried because of unreasonable demands by the adverse party, then a good working relationship between attorney and client is indispensable for successful litigation. The lawyer must understand the client and must perceive the nuances of the marital conflict in order to present the case effectively and to anticipate the strategies of opposing counsel.

Let me suggest some questions to consider in analyzing your interviewing and counseling performance, especially in matrimonial practice.

1. What is your objective? When you first meet a client, your main goal should be to start establishing an effective lawyer-client relationship. You must win the client's confidence and trust, and begin to develop an understanding of the client and his problems. Such a relationship will enable you to prepare well for necessary court appearances and to negotiate an ultimate resolution of the case with the attorney for the adverse spouse. Establishing and maintaining that sort of relationship requires far more than fact-gathering. Joe Friday—with his "Just the facts, Ma'am," style—would have been a poor divorce lawyer.

2. Are you a good listener? The essence of interviewing is listening. Good listening means paying real attention and resisting the temptation to interrupt frequently, but it means far more. When interviewing a divorce client, the lawyer should practice "active listening,"[1] a technique by which you let the

---

[1] D. Binder & S. Price, LEGAL INTERVIEWING AND COUNSELING: A CLIENT CENTERED APPROACH 21–36 (1977); T. Shaffer, LEGAL INTERVIEWING AND COUNSELING IN A NUTSHELL 105–36 (1976); Barkai, *Active Listening*, 20 TRIAL 66 (Aug., 1984); Barkai, *How to Develop the Skill of Active Listening*, 30

client know that you hear and understand what he or she is telling you. It is a way of encouraging the client to give you information and to express feelings about the other spouse and the client's problems.[2]

A passive listener simply sits and takes notes as the client talks. This behavior makes the lawyer seem distant and uninterested in the substance of the client's problem. The passive lawyer never makes eye contact or speaks except to clarify details like the date of the marriage or the birth date of a child. She gives the client no chance to make human contact with her. She allows the client to ramble on with no sense of whether useful information is being provided.[3]

Passive listening is a common fault of young, inexperienced lawyers who believe they have to write down everything a client says from the beginning of the initial interview. Because note-taking interferes so directly with establishing a relationship, the lawyer should permit the client to tell his story in some detail before reaching for the note pad. While scribbling notes, the lawyer is missing the opportunity for a fuller and more useful understanding of the client and his situation, because the way the client presents himself and his story is important in the lawyer's assessment of the case.

Instead of writing notes about details that can easily be filled in later in the interview, listen actively and learn about your client's feelings and motivations; learn about the facts as the client chooses to tell them. Concentrate on establishing your relationship first, then go back and tie down specific, detailed factual material.[4]

Problems can also arise when the lawyer asks specific, di-

PRAC. LAW. 73 (June 1, 1984); Barkai & Fine, *Empathy Training for Lawyers and Law Students*, 13 Sw. U. L. REV. 505 (1983).

[2]Binder & Price, *supra*, at 25.

[3]*See* Barkai, *Active Listening*, 20 TRIAL 66, 67 (Aug. 1984); D. Binder & S. Price, *supra*, note 1 at 23–24.

[4]Howarth & Hetrick, 9 Litigation 25, 26 (Summer, 1983); Schoenfield & Schoenfield, *The Art of Interviewing and Counseling*, in THE PRACTICAL LAWYER'S MANUAL ON LAWYER-CLIENT RELATIONS, 1, 6–7 (1983); D. Binder & S. Price, *supra*, note 1 at 59–79.

rective questions and rigidly controls the interview, a technique that prevents real, human contact with the client. The questions may be read from a questionnaire or may be recited from the memory of countless such interviews, and the lawyer employing this strategy is likely to be taking notes, or using a tape recorder.

The directive, controlling lawyer is likely to get only the information he asks for. As the client perceives it, the lawyer knows what is important and has no time for other matters. The client may even experience some rebuke, subtle or otherwise, when she volunteers information not directly responsive to the lawyer's question.

Directive behavior will be necessary with all clients at some times during the lawyer-client relationship, and some clients require far more control than others. With nearly all clients, however, it is best not to be directive early in the first interview, which is a critical time in the lawyer-client relationship, a time to practice active listening.[5]

As an active listener you reflect back what the client says, showing the client that you understand what you have heard. You acknowledge feelings expressed by the client as well as facts. The client tells his story with minimal interference. By listening actively, occasionally restating facts or recognizing and accepting feelings, you show that you care about the client, his problem, and his feelings.[6] It is only after establishing rapport and getting a sense of the situation that you should take out a legal pad and write down the specific information you need. Both you and your client will be surprised and pleased at how well you will remember most of the information from the client's monologue.

---

[5]The client in a highly emotional state may need a more structured interviewing style. *See* Schoenfield & Schoenfield, *How to Handle a Client in a State of Crisis*, in THE PRACTICAL LAWYER'S MANUAL ON LAWYER-CLIENT RELATIONS, 105, 107–08 (1983).

[6]For a good discussion of the benefits of active listening, which the authors also refer to as "empathic communications skills," *see* Barkai & Fine, *Empathy Training for Lawyers and Law Students*, 13 Sw. U. L. REV. 505, 510–17 (1983).

It is easier to reflect facts than feelings. As you collect details about the couple's finances, it will often be useful to restate some of the data, rather than passively writing it down. Often you will do this automatically when you direct the client to give more information on the same subject: "Your husband makes $30,000 working for Acme Industries. What exactly does he do there?" The preface to your question shows that you heard and understood the last answer.

Active listening will help you to focus on a particular topic and cover it well before moving on. At the same time it will let the client know that he is being heard and understood and will enable him to correct any misimpressions immediately.[7]

3. Do you encourage your clients to ventilate feelings? Recognizing the client's feelings and reflecting them back is even more important. Suppose that a woman says, "My husband left me, and I don't know how I'm going to manage." That statement calls for more than a question like, "When did he leave?" Even worse would be, "Why did he leave?" Her statement calls for acknowledgment of her emotions: "He's gone and you're feeling overwhelmed." Such a response tells the client that her feelings as well as her facts are significant. The response allows her to elaborate on her emotions, giving the lawyer an opportunity to learn what her critical, immediate needs are and to begin to explore ways of dealing with the separation over the long term.

Divorce clients bring their emotional problems to your office. If you are unwilling to hear about feelings, you are in the wrong business. Unless you understand your client's feelings, you are likely to try to fit him and his problem into an inappropriate package. How can you propose settlement of custody and property rights without a real understanding of your client's feelings about himself, his spouse, his children, and his finances?

A few years ago, I invited a psychiatrist to a law school class to discuss interviewing. A student asked what he should do if a client began to cry. The psychiatrist replied, "Offer the client

---

[7]*See* Barkai, *supra,* note 3 at 67.

a Kleenex and wait." The student was looking for an easy way to avoid his own discomfort. The doctor urged him to recognize his discomfort and to permit, even to encourage, the client to express emotions.[8]

Therapists developed active listening to permit and encourage patients or clients to express their feelings. Lawyers should stop looking for ways to prevent clients from doing just that. Changing the subject, making promises to "take care of things," or saying "I know how you feel" are frequent tactics to avoid listening to client feelings. If you catch yourself using those or other avoidance tactics, change your approach.

Anger is one of the most common emotions that clients feel in the divorce process. If you do not permit a client to express anger at the spouse or if you stifle an emotional outburst prematurely, you may find that the client's anger and hostility continues far longer than you think it should. You might even replace the spouse as the person about whom the client would say, "He doesn't give a damn how I feel."

Active listening does not require you to share the client's emotion or to approve of it. It does require that you accept the feelings being expressed and let the client know it. It is tempting to say, "I understand," or "I know how you feel," but the client in pain knows you cannot feel the pain or understand it. Such a statement may cause resentment or provoke an angry response. You must accept the client's feelings in a nonjudgmental way. It is just as wrong to say, "You have every right to be angry at your spouse," as it is to say, "Don't be so hostile." You should not side with the client who expresses anger at the spouse, but instead you must recognize the anger and accept it. When you say, "You're very angry," you identify the emotional state of the client and show a willingness to accept it and to permit the client to express it.[9]

---

[8] Recognition and acceptance of client feelings is critically important. So is the lawyer's reaction. He must "level with the client about the *lawyer's* feelings." T. Shaffer, *supra* note 1, at 35–39.

[9] *See* Mulhare, *How to Handle a New Client: A Psychodynamic Approach*, in THE PRACTICAL LAWYER'S MANUAL ON LAWYER-CLIENT RELATIONS, 29, 32 (1983).

4. Are you judgmental? Few things can more seriously damage the attorney-client relationship than a lawyer's judgmental attitude.[10] If you show disapproval of the emotions the client expresses or of the client's conduct, you may cut off information on sensitive topics; you may lose the client altogether. If, on the other hand, you approve of the client's anger at the spouse, you may increase or prolong the fighting between them and contribute to a settlement impasse. The active listener reflects the feelings of the client nonjudgmentally and will be seen as someone who cares, someone to trust.

5. Do you control your clients or contract with them? It would be easier if our clients would follow our advice without question or argument, but that is too much to expect. In the divorce process and in legal matters generally, the basic decisions belong to the client: whether to accept a settlement offer or go to trial is certainly a client decision. The ultimate client decision is, should I fire my lawyer and hire someone else? Whatever you think about your control of the client, you could be surprised when the time comes to present a settlement.

Because the major decisions are for the client to make, with your advice, it is important to begin early to show the client that the relationship is a partnership in which the client must participate actively. You need to contract with the client[11]: to establish a clear working agreement. Help her to see what she can and must do for herself without your help; encourage her to take responsibility for resolving her own problems. Some lawyers ask the client to write a summary of the marital history or to collect and organize information about financial

---

[10]Shaffer urges lawyers to avoid judging the client and engaging in what he calls "evaluative counseling." T. Shaffer, *supra*, note 1 at 133–36. If the lawyer reveals a judgmental attitude, the client may withhold information because he may feel that a truthful response will lead the lawyer to think negatively of him. Some questions pose an ego threat—a threat to the client's self-esteem. D. Binder & S. Price, *supra*, note 1 at 10.

[11]Shaffer, *supra*, note 1 at 106–16; Schoenfield & Schoenfield, *How to Handle a Client in a State of Crisis*, in THE PRACTICAL LAYWER'S MANUAL ON LAWYER-CLIENT RELATIONS 105, 112–13 (1983).

matters. Your client, especially if she has children, must learn to deal with the other spouse without your help. If you impose decisions on her rather than helping her work through the issues, you will lose the chance to teach her how to make her own decisions and to work out post-divorce problems without you[12]. Besides, the more dependent a client is, the more headaches and telephone calls you will get.

One of the benefits of active listening is that it promotes the development of the contract between lawyer and client. The lawyer is not the dominant, aggressive questioner but a willing, nonjudgmental listener. As the case proceeds, the lawyer should be teaching the client that the lawyer cares and can help, but that the ultimate solution requires the client's active participation and assent.

6. *Do you know what time it is?* One objective must be to help turn the client's attention away from the past and toward the future.[13] Often that means the client must give up the idea of revenge or compensation for past wrongs and face the future as a single person and perhaps as a custodial or noncustodial parent. This reorientation occurs naturally for many divorce clients and does not require much help from the lawyer; in that case, the familiar medical maxim, "First Do No Harm," should be observed. Judging the other spouse when your client expresses anger is a way to demonstrate partisanship, but it is the wrong way. Active listening gives support without encouraging revenge.

Many experienced divorce lawyers have found that divorce clients go through stages like those experienced by the terminally ill.[14] The first reaction may be denial—an unrealistic belief that reconciliation will occur. Then most divorce clients

---

[12]*See* Grana, *Post-Divorce Counseling: A Process for Implementing the Role of Separate-but-Joint Parent*, 21 J. FAM. L. 687, 688–90 (1982–83).

[13]*Id.* at 688–91, 701–02; Hancock, *The Power of the Attorney in Divorce*, 19 J. FAM. L. 235, 242–43.

[14]*See* E. Kubler-Ross, ON DEATH AND DYING (1969). Compare the stages described in that book with the stages of the divorce process as described in Grana, *supra*, note 12 at 691–96.

PREPARING THE CLIENT

go through an anger stage. They are angry about being left alone and may direct their anger at the spouse or displace it and direct it at others, including the children and the lawyer. Many clients experience depression. Finally, the client who works through the process successfully will enter a stage of acceptance in which he will be prepared to face life as a single person and perhaps as a single custodial or noncustodial parent. That client will be ready to work out an appropriate settlement.

If you know what stage of the divorce process your client is in, you will be able to react appropriately. A client in the denial stage will be unprepared to make a settlement because he will be unable to face the permanent loss of the spouse. A client in the anger stage will be unwilling to settle because she will feel the need to demand the last ounce of revenge. A depressed client might want to accept a poor settlement just to avoid further stress.

In addition, you need to perceive what stage of the process the adverse party is in. If opposing counsel is purposely or inadvertently keeping his client focused on revenge for past behavior, you will have to delay the negotiation process and postpone all but absolutely necessary hearings. If you and your client avoid aggravating behavior, the adverse spouse eventually may press her lawyer to seek settlement, or if you are lucky may change to a more skillful, reasonable attorney. In a case like this it will also be beneficial to seek the assistance of a third party: a judge, mediator, or referee who, unlike you, may be able to deal directly with the adverse spouse and help with the reorientation process.

7. *Do you know when and how to refer clients for therapy?* Even lawyers who are exceptionally good at active listening and who take time to allow clients to express feelings must refer some clients for therapy. Lawyers lack the training and experience to practice psychotherapy. Active listening has some therapeutic benefits but should not be seen as a substitute for therapy. It merely enables the lawyer to do his job well and permits the client to work through the divorce process. Clients who do not

progress, and those whose emotional distress seems most serious, need to be referred to a therapist.[15]

A client should not be referred to therapy simply because the lawyer is unwilling to take time to listen to his expression of feelings. Many clients will be reluctant to face the need to see a therapist. If you attempt a referral before you have established your own willingness to listen and have shown that you care about the client and his problems, the client is likely to see the referral as a slough-off. That damages the lawyer-client relation, perhaps irreparably, and makes it far less likely that the client will go for needed help. If you have been judgmental about the client's behavior or feelings, he may fear that you think he is crazy. Sound interviewing and counseling techniques enable the lawyer to sort out and refer those clients who need therapy.

8. Do you have difficulty discussing fees? Few lawyers do *not* have difficulty dealing with fees in the divorce interview. First, there are practical problems. It is not possible, at the first interview, to know how much work will be involved. At best you can explain your hourly rate, your retainer, and how you will bill the client for time worked. Moreover, fee discussions are awkward for inexperienced lawyers because they are not confident that their services are worth the price they must state. They try to pass over the issue quickly, and they react defensively when the client seeks more information or says he cannot afford that much. Veteran practitioners tend to state the fee in a firm, take-it-or-leave-it way, but they too exhibit some defensiveness about fees. They may be quite confident that their services are worth the price, but they are unsure that the client will agree.

The interviewing techniques described above, especially active listening, will not eliminate your discomfort in explaining your fees. The techniques will, however, enable your client to see you as a person who cares. That can make a world of difference in the client's willingness to pay.

---

[15] D. Binder & S. Price, *supra* note 1 at 211–23; Schoenfield & Schoenfield, *How to Handle a Client in a State of Crisis*, in THE PRACTICAL LAWYER'S MANUAL ON LAWYER-CLIENT RELATIONS 105, 113–14 (1983).

PREPARING THE CLIENT

9. Can you make your own luck? Early in my practice, I saw a client who had been battling with her husband in domestic relations court for several years. Because of the now-abandoned doctrine of recrimination, she had been able to prevent her husband from divorcing her to marry another woman. She was obviously angry because of his infidelity, and that anger had lasted for years. At least four earlier lawyers had represented her and each had recommended settlement. She could have had custody, reasonable support and alimony, and the family home. Each time settlement was offered, she refused to give her husband a divorce and fired the lawyer who had recommended settlement.

When she came to my office, she had just been discharged from a psychiatric hospital. While she was in the institution, her husband had obtained a court order placing the children with his parents in another state. He had also obtained an *ex parte* divorce in Florida and had married the other woman. My client had never received any alimony or support money and the bank had foreclosed and sold the home. She had spent several thousand dollars in legal fees.

During one of several lengthy interviews, she revealed that she had refused to permit the divorce because she expected to inherit a large sum from her husband's parents. She thought that the marital relation gave her inheritance rights in their estates. I asked who told her that. She said she just knew it.

Why had this misunderstanding gone uncorrected so long? Anger seemed to be the obvious explanation for her refusal to permit the divorce. None of the prior attorneys could have thought to ask about this sort of motivation. Because it indicated greed, it was not something she would readily volunteer. Luck, rather than skill, led me to this information. The incident convinced me that, although my time is valuable, a lot of serious listening is necessary to represent divorce clients well.

CHAPTER THREE

The Art and Craft of Successful Divorce Negotiation

Gary N. Skoloff

Even though few divorce cases reach trial, most lawyers devote their time and effort to the study of litigation techniques and tactics, leaving the technique of negotiation an orphaned craft. They learn about negotiation on the job without realizing that negotiation techniques are part of a coherent system of study. This chapter will touch on basic principles and then will discuss practical points to consider when preparing for negotiations, strategies negotiators can use, and negotiation ethics.

PRINCIPLES OF NEGOTIATION

Know Your Client and Your Client's Objectives

Proper client representation means understanding your client's goals. By properly understanding these goals, the attorney may be able to separate his client's needs from issues that are being communicated to him by nonparty outsiders. Third parties often attend your meetings with the client, and it is important to separate these persons' needs from your client's goals. The stepchild, business partner, or cohabitor of your client may have needs and goals contrary to those of your client. Their goals may be affecting the client's demands.

By having a client address these issues head on, the attorney can better understand the motivation behind the client's goals and help the client measure the options. It is important for the attorney to educate the client about domestic relations law and the procedures of divorce litigation. If third parties are involved "behind the scenes," the attorney should make a strong effort to educate these interlopers as well. They can often be a troublesome stumbling block to a negotiated settlement. However, they can sometimes be helpful to settlement if they maintain a dispassionate point of view.

The Need for Complete Disclosure

It is absolutely essential that the attorney fully understand the circumstances of the litigation before commencing negotiations with the other side. One cannot negotiate from a position of ignorance.

In matrimonial litigation, this means that all assets subject to equitable distribution must be identified and valued. The income and earning capacity of each party must be determined. If custody or visitation is an issue, evaluations of the parties and their children must be completed, and each party must express to his or her attorney the factual basis for his or her position.

Be an Effective Communicator

An attorney communicates both verbally and nonverbally. Your silence during a negotiation may be as telling as a wink or a blush. The tone of your voice, a rapid eye movement, a perspiring forehead, or a cold hand may signify a reaction. As lawyers we may try to minimize our communication of such cues. But clients may be less able to control their appearance and expressions. Be cognizant of the client's weaknesses. If a client cannot control himself, don't bring him to negotiation sessions.

Effective communication involves discussing a client's position in terms of interests, goals, and policy, rather than voicing demands that seek to take advantage of the parties' personal deficiencies. The positions taken should be explained—how were they arrived at, and how are each of the client's needs being met? Before discussing specific proposals, the needs of each party should be explored so that appropriate demands and offers can be made by the attorneys.

It should also be noted, in line with nonverbal communication, that negotiations in a small conference room with people seated at a small, round table will be more likely to open up discussion than negotiations in a formal setting, which tend to stifle open discussion and cause participants to resist flexible thinking.

Developing a Strategy

Developing a plan is important in successfully negotiating a matter to resolution. Your plan will, of course, depend upon your client's goals. For negotiations over custody and visitation, you may need to develop a cooperative attitude because the parties will be compelled to deal with each other after the divorce. Being combative may help you obtain an advantageous financial result, but in the custody area it can spell disaster if the parties become unable to communicate with each other after the divorce.

Attorneys who have a full understanding of their clients' goals will be successful negotiators because they will be able to set priorities for their objectives. As a general rule, if the most important demands cannot be settled at the beginning of the negotiations, the desire to compromise will be directly proportionate to the amount of time invested.

PREPARATIONS FOR NEGOTIATION

Even after each negotiator has gathered the necessary factual information, several questions must be resolved before negotiations begin.

Where Should the Negotiations Take Place?

Everyone understands that in sports the home team has an advantage over the visiting team. Is this true in negotiations?

Many times it will work to your advantage to be the visiting team in a negotiation. As the visitor you limit the amount of information that you bring to the meeting. If there is information that you do not wish to discuss, you can always tell your adversary that you did not bring your entire file and do not have the information readily available. It is impossible to make this excuse credibly when the meeting is held at your own office. In addition, if you or your client is perceived as "high-powered," going to your adversary's office with "hat in hand," serves to equalize the stature of the attorneys. The less powerful attorney may feel more comfortable and be less on guard. Appearing at someone else's office also makes that lawyer the host, which requires him or her to be gracious, to offer you coffee or a soft drink, perhaps to provide food during the meeting. The home team is transformed from adversary to host.

As the visitor, you are in a better position to conclude the negotiations than your adversary. If the negotiations are held in your office, you cannot throw yourself out or walk out the door. As host, you have to be polite. If you are the visitor and things are not going well, you may conclude the negotiations by storming out of your adversary's office or politely saying that you have another appointment and must leave immediately.

Should the Client Be Present?

Whether negotiations demand the client's presence depends on your strategy. Success may flow from "bad mouthing" the client as unreasonable, illogical, or difficult. One viable negotiation technique is to keep placing blame on the client, causing the other side to continue making concessions. You can hardly take this approach if your client is present.

On the other hand, the client's presence may be helpful when the attorney takes on the role of "mad dog." Your client can then turn to the spouse and apologize for your lack of control. Concessions and or apologies that appear to be made over the attorney's objections may restore good will between the parties and allow them to resolve the issues quickly to prevent the attorney from becoming a runaway train.

The lawyer must also consider the psychological makeup of the client. A client who cannot control his or her facial expressions, for example, may damage your credibility as a negotiator. There is nothing more destructive than a client whose reactions undermine your ability to negotiate.

The Timing of Negotiations

Timing is important, in relation to the overall care and even with respect to the time of day.

In early stages of negotiations, one side may be more willing than the other to negotiate rather than expend substantial sums on attorneys and experts. The husband, for example, might be dealing from strength as the repository of financial information necessary to determine the value of the assets. That is one compelling reason why, from the wife's perspective, negotiations should not take place until discovery has been completed (but negotiation sessions may be used as informal proceedings to obtain such disclosure). On the other hand, a wife may not have any incentive to negotiate when she retains exclusive occupancy of the marital residence, receives substantial support, and does not work.

With respect to the time of day, a negotiation that begins at 8:30 a.m. will undoubtedly last longer than one starting at 4:00 p.m. Friday. It may actually be to your benefit to commence negotiations on the Friday afternoon preceding your Monday trial date. It depends on your position and strength.

You must also consider whether you are a morning, afternoon, or evening person. You will want to negotiate when your physical and intellectual strength is at its peak. If you are generally wiped out by 5:00 in the afternoon, it will be to your advantage to commence negotiations in the early morning—especially if you know that your adversary is a late riser.

Creating the Right Ambiance

The environment in which you negotiate should be conducive to settlement. If the negotiations are to proceed on a friendly basis, the room should be warm and intimate. It may be better to sit at a round table or side by side at the front of your desk than at a large conference table on opposite sides or to have your adversary sit in a chair across from your desk, giving the appearance that you are dictating to him or her.

Food and beverages should be provided to all participants. The concept of breaking bread with your enemy is important in creating the right atmosphere.

Sometimes negotiations should be held at a neutral site. Negotiations at the courthouse take place in aura of formality and allow participants to feel that they have had their "day in court." On the other hand, negotiations in a restaurant over lunch may promote cooperative and conciliatory behavior.

STRATEGIES

Passive vs. Aggressive Behavior

The literature of negotiation indicates no relationship between aggressiveness and effective negotiation. Apparently, aggressives cause reactions that stifle conciliation. An aggressive is likely to bring out anger and embarrassment in the opponent, which may cause the opponent to fight harder and hold out. Nevertheless aggressiveness is an important tool that can highlight the unreasonableness of your adversary's position. An aggressive reaction may cause the adversary to reconsider his or her position or back down. You should not get caught up in an aggressive's game plan but should insist on returning to the agenda at hand.

Gamesmanship: How to Offer, How to Bargain

It is always desirable to have your opponent make the first offer. It is just as important that your reaction be immediate and sincere. If the first offer is outrageous, your outrage should be immediately communicated to your adversary, otherwise it will not be believed.

Customarily, the first demand is unrealistic and is used merely to commence the "real negotiations." In that context you should explain the reasons for demands when communicating them. You should clearly state, in setting forth an opening position, why your client is entitled to the relief sought. If your adversary does not provide you with an explanation for his or her position, demand one, and do not be afraid to ask for detailed information and objective reasons in support of that position.

In shaping a counterproposal or compromise, it is important to determine the real interests of the parties and then to fashion relief that satisfies competing interests to the maximum extent. Once this has been done, you should communicate to your adversary the reasons for your position and the benefits to his or her client.

Emotions and Threats

Threats can be used in resolving disputes. Never make a threat, however, unless you fully intend to carry it out and are capable of doing so. A threat must be believed to be effective. A husband who threatens to disappear from the face of the earth to avoid paying alimony may not be believed when putting such a threat into practice would be too risky. Yet, a threat that the husband may lose his job as a result of the preparation requirements for a contested divorce may present sufficient reason for the wife to begin negotiating cooperatively. A threat of litigation or appeal may convince the other spouse to negotiate in good faith. However, threats are never appropriate if negotiations commence under duress or the result is based on fraud.

If you or your client are threatened during negotiations, the best response is to laugh or ask that the statement be repeated. If you are silent you will appear to consider the threat believable.

Interpreting Reactions

You should carefully observe the reactions of your adversary (and his or her client if present) during negotiations. Spontaneous reactions are telltale signs of what they are actually thinking.

You should also keep track of all concessions. Their sequence may reliably predict the settlement point, since many negotiators expect concessions to be made in patterns.

Your adversary may respond with humor. While a joke can lighten up the negotiations, jocularity may indicate poor judgment, lack of sensitivity to the issues, or an inability to treat negotiations seriously. Humor may also be used as a diversionary tactic to avoid addressing an issue.

Dealing with Deadlocks

Deadlocks, which can occur at any time, can be exasperating. The parties will feel a greater sense of loss if they have been negotiating in good faith for long periods because much of their investment will be lost. You should try to meet each block head-on in order to break through to progress. Search areas that both sides agree on. The parties may at least be able to agree that their interests or needs will not be served by deadlock. From there, they may discuss their relative positions and the serious effects of failing to settle.

At a time of deadlock, the parties can agree to take a short break or to reconsider the deadlock positions last and move on to a new topic. Moving closer to settlement in other areas can foster additional good faith and willingness to compromise.

One possibility is to split the difference. That step should be taken only as a last resort after all issues have been narrowed and resolved to the extent possible. Without such narrowing, the cost of this resolution cannot be determined.

Of course, the ultimate step is to stage a walkout. Before taking such a drastic step, you must consider the effects. A walkout might mean the end of any communication between the respective parties and at the least will cause escalation of each party's emotional state.

NEGOTIATION ETHICS

Lying and Manipulation

As officers of the court, attorneys must be careful in their statements during negotiations. Lawyers must deal fairly with others. We are prohibited from engaging in dishonesty, deceit, or fraud. Nor can we knowingly permit clients to perpetuate a fraud. We are obligated to rectify and correct the wrongs we learn about.

The conduct of a negotiator and even silence may cause the other side to make erroneous inferences. Yet, puffing and exaggeration are expected in the negotiation process. It is certainly ethical to take a position or express your opinion during negotiations. You must walk a very thin line.

Authority Issues

The lawyer must clearly understand the extent of his or her authority and not exceed it. As the agent of your client, you must be careful not to bind the client beyond the scope of your authority.

Errors & Omissions

Do not have an ego problem during negotiations. Admit the limited nature of your authority or quickly admit an error so that the mistake is not compounded by reliance on the initial statement.

Other dangers to avoid include failure to communicate offers to your client, failure to propose recommendations or explain alternatives, and making unauthorized offers to one's opponent. Failure to take care of the reasonable requests of your client can subject you to a malpractice suit.

CHAPTER FOUR
The Four-Way Negotiation Conference
Roberta F. Benjamin

Negotiation in the matrimonial context, although featuring certain traditional elements, is highly specialized and requires of attorneys a unique range of skills and insights. This is because divorce disputes are so heavily laden with intense emotion and the issues strike at the most private and vulnerable of human concerns. Love, attachment, rejection, security, abandonment—strong feelings about all of these run through matrimonial dissolution, a process that mental health professionals agree is one of the most traumatic of the modern human experience.

Unlike parties to a typical business transaction or civil litigation, parties to a divorce continue to be involved with each other in varying degrees after the legal issues have been laid to rest. Matrimonial practitioners must therefore bear in mind that the dynamics of divorce negotiation and the patterns of interaction established have repercussions for the restructured family for many years to come.

One of the services a skillful matrimonial practitioner can perform is to provide a negotiation process that encourages both parties to articulate genuine concerns, listen to and acknowledge the other side's concerns, and move forward with realistic future planning. Attorneys in a divorce negotiation often serve as role models for their clients in the area of problem-solving. Most clients, after all, are novices in divorce and divorce negotiation, and if they were skillful at negotiating in an emotionally charged context, would not be seeking help from an attorney. An effective attorney teaches by example how to negotiate and enables the client to learn and use negotiating skills. This enabling function is a combination of sharing insights, encouragement, and demystification of the process.

Perhaps the ideal way to achieve long-range resolution in a matrimonial case is the four-way negotiation conference, in which the parties and their attorneys meet to share concerns and solve problems.

WHY A FOUR-WAY CONFERENCE?

As noted above, divorcing couples are often not effective in negotiating with each other. The four-way conference, with skillful attorneys serving as role models, can begin to establish negotiation skills that will have a long-term impact on the parties' post-divorce life. Moreover, the clients' involvement gives them a sense of control and direct participation in fashioning the terms of their settlement. If both parties perceive that they have shaped the agreement, both have a stake in living up to its terms. Post-divorce legal problems and lack of compliance with the terms of a settlement most often result when one party feels or both feel that attorneys controlled or manipulated the process and shut them out.

When the four-way session is planned and experienced as a joint problem-solving meeting, it can also lay to rest many of the couple's fears and serve as a reality base for the parties of their counsel. For example, if the wife is perceiving that the husband's attorney is listening to her concerns and responding to them, she may feel less anxious and more willing to explore options. And the wife's attorney may modify his or her views about the case if that attorney—who has heard about the husband only through the skewed descriptions of an angry client—can see the husband not as a scheming Lothario but as a decent individual going through a time of crisis.

The four-way meeting, then, provides all participants with information and insights about the concerns, needs, and unique quirks of the others. It also serves to underscore the reality that resolution of a divorce involves at least *four* individuals, restructuring the lives of *two*.

WHEN NOT TO USE FOUR-WAY NEGOTIATION

The four-way conference is not a panacea. Whatever its benefits when successful, the process is not to be recommended: (1) if one party (either your client or the spouse) is inappropriately angry or vindictive for a prolonged period or is extremely rigid and unable to compromise; (2) if there has been a significant history of physical abuse in the marriage; or (3) when opposing counsel is inexperienced or abusive. In those circumstances, it is unlikely that the negotiation process will achieve the desired goals and the most efficient and least emotionally draining course is to move the matter to trial.

WHEN TO HOLD A NEGOTIATION CONFERENCE

While the four-way negotiation conference can occur at any point it is usually held at some point of crisis or as a deadline looms near—either a judicially imposed deadline (because a hearing on temporary orders, a pretrial conference, or the trial itself is imminent) or an emotionally imposed deadline (because the parties or attorneys feel a distinct need for closure and resolution). Typically, a conference prior to a hearing on temporary orders produces limited information on limited issues. The focus here will be on those conferences held at the later stages, when discovery (either formal or informal) is complete and the parties have made preliminary proposals. At this later point, the issues to be negotiated have been defined.

If the goal of the conference is to try to reach a final resolution, the ideal timing will vary from case to case and, in significant measure, will depend on the emotional stage at which the client has arrived (and the spouse as well). Broadly considered, there appear to be several emotional stages of divorce. The initial stage is often described as a "holding on" period, characterized by resistance (to accepting responsibility for marital problems, or to physical change of any sort), ambivalence, depression, preoccupation with the past, and a low energy level. A client whose focus is on the past, who seems passive, who shifts positions and refuses to consider changes in lifestyle or environment, is in the holding on stage. He or she is in extreme and often appropriate distress. When either spouse is holding on, the time is not ripe to attempt to negotiate a final settlement. Indeed, a four-way conference at this point may be an expensive and frustrating waste of energy and may set the case back by months.

The next emotional stage is the "letting go" period. Resistance decreases, the focus moves to the present, and the individual's energy level increases. Anger often replaces depression, but there is tentativeness and some confusion.

In the third stage of the emotional process, the individual is "getting on with it." Attachments to the former spouse and lifestyle begin to diminish, the individual is oriented toward the present and the immediate future, and the energy level is high.

The final stage, stabilization, typically occurs after the divorce. Behavior patterns include confidence in decision-making, an orientation that integrates past, present, and future, and a positive exploration of new lifestyles.

Because matrimonial attorneys seldom see final-stage clients, the negotiation process is most often fruitful in the latter part of the letting go stage and in the getting-on-with-it period. As a general guideline, you can expect that nine months after separation, the parties will have experienced the highly emotional initial stages, accepted the reality of divorce, and developed the ability to look toward the future; they are likely to be ready to focus on post-divorce planning.

Ideal timing is largely intuitive, and intuition derives from experience, knowledge of the client, and a sense of the other side. One spouse may have quickly gone through the initial stages, moved into a new relationship, and be ready to settle the case. That puts pressure on the attorney to move the case quickly. If the other spouse has been shocked by the separation and needs more time to adjust, it is in everyone's best interest to wait until the situation stabilizes before attempting a finalizing conference. Resolutions arrived at because one party feels guilty and is ready to give too much, and the other party is baffled and confused, seldom produce effective long-term settlements.

WHERE TO HOLD THE CONFERENCE

Probably the most pressured and, unfortunately, most common four-way conferences are held at the courthouse. Sitting on a public bench with a yellow pad trying to negotiate and finalize an agreement between divorcing spouses is frustrating for the attorney, demeaning for the parties, and intensely stressful for everyone involved. It should be avoided.

The better location is in the offices of one of the attorneys. As a strategic question, "your place or mine?" has no right answer. There are advantages and disadvantages to both. According to the accepted view, it is advantageous to have the other side come to your offices because you will have more control of the situation, and you and your client can feel secure and comfortable. However, there may be times when meeting at opposing counsel's office is good strategy. You can control the duration—you can leave opposing counsel's office, but it is more awkward to leave your own or terminate a session in your own. If you have large, elegant offices and opposing counsel does not, that lawyer may feel intimidated by your surroundings and tend to respond by being tougher or more aggressive than he or she would be in his or her own, more modest quarters.

HOW MANY CONFERENCES?

Assuming that both sides are satisfied with the financial information available and that written proposals and counter-proposals have been exchanged, one or two four-way conferences appear to be the norm. If one client seems or both seem to want or need more than that, it may well be time for both attorneys to look cooperatively and carefully at the dynamics of what is occurring. Typically they will see an inability to reach emotional closure. Perhaps a period of mediation or at least a cooling off period might be helpful. There are limits on what lawyers and the legal system can achieve in the divorce setting. If the four-way negotiation begins to take on the dynamics of a group therapy session, the parties should be guided toward more appropriate professionals.

PREPARATION FOR THE FOUR-WAY CONFERENCE

Since this usually will be a negotiation session under an emotional, pretrial, or trial deadline, and since deadlines in any negotiation context tend to produce concessions, preparation is important. The attorney should carefully review the proposals and go over them with the client. He or she should explore options and variations on the themes presented to date. Most important, the attorney should analyze the range of proposals against the backdrop of the likely outcome were the case to be tried. That outcome, as Roger Fisher and William Ury describe in *Getting To Yes*,[1] is the BATNA (Best Alternative To A Negotiated Agreement). This forms the standard against which any proposed settlement should be measured. As part of analyzing the case and the BATNA, it is also important to analyze and discuss with the client the trial costs to the family, not only the financial costs but also the long-term emotional costs.

---

[1] R. Fisher & W. Ury, GETTING TO YES (1981). *See* Chapter 1.

FOUR-WAY NEGOTIATION

In preparing the client for a conference, the attorney ought to give a clear preliminary analysis and explain its basis; he or she should point out the trouble spots and any possible areas of compromise and concession. If the negotiation team is to work well, attorney and client must share information.

Generally the client, no matter how sophisticated, will be wholly inexperienced in this sort of negotiation and typically feels inadequate, uncomfortable, and ill-informed.

In preparing the clients for a four-way negotiation session, it is critical to anticipate and acknowledge his or her fears directly and realistically. Humor often helps. As an example:

> I know this session is not something you're looking forward to, and often people are worried that some of their most private behavior will be exposed. It seldom happens.
> Last year, I recall, I had a client who was terrified that his wife would bring up his habit of eating potato chips in the bathtub. She never did. Turns out that when they talked later, she was equally frightened that he would talk about her various banana-and-grapefruit diets. The reality is that lawyers aren't interested in these details nor are judges. Attorney Jones, who is representing your wife, won't be at all interested in potato chips in or out of the tub, and . . ."

NEGOTIATION STYLE AND DYNAMICS

Style

Negotiation style is nowhere so apparent during a divorce case as in the four-way negotiation, in which the four participants are negotiating with each other on a range of levels. The literature divides lawyers as negotiators into two categories based on style, cooperative and competitive. Both can be effective, although the literature suggests that a higher percentage of effective negotiators use the cooperative style rather than the competitive. Common sense indicates that, when structuring a divorce agreement (as opposed to negotiating a tort case), the cooperative style is more appropriate. This is particularly true because one of the negotiation goals is to provide a post-divorce model of negotiation for the parties. Ability as a trial attorney appears to correlate to the effectiveness of both cooperative and competitive negotiators. Effective negotiators are good trial attorneys and are confident of that fact. The correlation makes sense, because the trial and its results are always in the background (as the BATNA), and an effective negotiator is not intimidated by the thought of going to trial.

Both types of negotiators, when effective, share certain characteristics, which include experience, honesty, integrity, rationality, thorough preparedness, self-control, intuition, and perception. Both types, when effective, observe the customs and courtesies of the bar and can be versatile and creative.

What are the differences in approach between the two styles? Broadly, the cooperative attorney, while desiring the best settlement for the client, also values fair settlement, meeting the client's needs, avoiding litigation, and maintaining or establishing a workable personal relationship with the other side. This attorney tends to begin with a realistic opening position, is forthright and flexible about the position, seeks to facilitate agreement, and avoids the use of threats. Fisher and Ury call this "principled negotiation" or "negotiation on the merits."[2] Such negotiation is particularly useful in the matrimonial setting, because a fair agreement and a process perceived as open are much more likely than the competitive alternative to produce the desired long-term result of post-divorce compliance.

The competitive negotiator tends to place a value on maximizing settlement for his or her own client and obtaining a profitable fee. Fair settlement is far less significant for the competitive atttorney than outdoing or outmaneuvering the opponent. The competitive negotiator tends to take an unrealistic opening position and uses threats as a tactic. He or she is viewed as far more rigid than the cooperative negotiator. As

---

[2]*Id.*

noted in Williams' *Legal Negotiation and Settlement*, reporting a study that forms the basis of the above comments, "Cooperatives feel that cases should be evaluated objectively, on their merits, and that both sides should seek to find the most fair outcome. Competitive attorneys view their work as a game in which they seek to outwit and outperform the other side."[3] Fisher and Ury call competitive negotiation "positional bargaining," which they view not only as inefficient but also as endangering ongoing relationships.

In preparing for a four-way negotiation conference, the attorney should be aware of his or her general style and that of opposing counsel. Two cooperative styles, even at different levels of experience, work well without great effort during a negotiation conference. Two competitive styles may also work well, if less comfortably. A mix of two different styles can result in an extremely stressful negotiation conference, particularly if the articulated goal of both *clients* is to achieve resolution. For example, the competitive attorney will often use threats, ridicule, or bluff as pressure tactics to achieve high levels of tension and win concessions. For example, the competitive attorney might say:

> Look, either my client gets sole custody and the house or we go to trial. Mister's girlfriend is going to be pretty embarrassed. I mean, a guy who leaves his wife and three kids for a woman who isn't even divorced yet! How do you think *her* custody battle is going to go if we haul her into court?

When faced with such tactics, an experienced, cooperative attorney may well respond by refusing to continue the negotiations. The result is an impasse.

Competitive attorneys may be well-advised to modify their strategy in the four-way negotiation, given the high risk of backfiring. Moreover, a cooperative attorney when anticipating a conference with a competitive type, should carefully

---

[3] G. Williams, LEGAL NEGOTIATION AND SETTLEMENT 25 (1983).

explain to the client what is likely to occur. If unprepared, that client is likely to doubt the attorney's "toughness" in the face of a vigorous, competitive onslaught. Prepared, the client can observe the dynamics more realistically and remain positive about the abilities and control of the cooperative attorney.

Dynamics

The dynamics of a four-way divorce negotiation are intense, delicate, and complex. The two parties confronting each other have lived in an intimate relationship, sometimes for years, know each other's vulnerabilities, and often continue to have mixed, strong feelings about each other. Because of the emotionally charged nature of the marriage relationship and its end, matrimonial attorneys have a special obligation to restrain their own egos and to focus on problem-solving. Deescalation of past conflict is often a major role attorneys should play. This is not to suggest that "venting" is inappropriate, but rather that both attorneys have a responsibility to listen, not overreact, and move the negotiation forward.

The model of negotiation suggested by Fisher and Ury, "principled negotiation" or "negotiation on the merits," is a particularly useful model for the divorce negotiation process and the four-way negotiation conference. Briefly, "principled negotiation" encourages (1) focusing on basic *interests*, not positions; (2) defining problems objectively and separating the people from the problem; and (3) inventing and looking at a *range* of options and possible solutions. The goal of principled negotiation is an amicable, efficient process and a wise agreement.

Attorneys can take on a range of roles in this setting. They negotiate, interpret their own clients's concerns and the opposing side's concerns, mediate, and define and redefine the problems. Below is an example of an interpretative comment by an attorney attempting to perform a responsible role:

> We seem to have been going 'round in circles for a bit. Let me try something. Jim says that he's willing to pay alimony,

but he wants to see a light at the end of the tunnel. In six years, he wants no further obligations and wants to make plans to cut back on his workload and maybe even change careers. Sally seems to acknowledge the validity of that, but she is concerned that she won't be able to earn sufficient income in six years. That seems to me to be a not unreasonable fear—Sally, after all, hasn't worked outside the home for 21 years and she's 49. You'd acknowledge that fear as legitimate, wouldn't you Jim? Okay.

Now, we do have the house and it has an equity of some $300,000.00. Jim has said Sally can live there for as long as she wants, even after the kids are in college, which is very decent. And I want to acknowledge that, Jim. Suppose we play with the idea that in six years Sally were to sell the house and have *use* of the proceeds to provide an income . . ."

The attorney has acknowledged and legitimized the concerns of both parties and set the negotiation on a track of exploring options. If the parties themselves can begin to negotiate this way, their post-divorce relationship (when their attorneys are not present) will be much smoother.

The following outline highlights some of the key concepts of "negotiation on the merits" as more fully detailed in *Getting To Yes*, and is useful to bear in mind and to share with the client:

Separate the People from the Problem

Negotiators (clients *and* attorneys) are people with emotions, values, viewpoints, and different backgrounds. In a negotiation, particularly a divorce negotiation, two kinds of interests need to be addressed—the substantive interest (the terms of the agreement) and the relationship interest. When these interests get entangled, agreement becomes difficult. It is therefore important to be continually alert to separate the relationship problems from the substantive problems. "People problems" fall into several broad categories—perception, involvement, communication, and emotion.

Perception. How people view the situation. This is not necessarily objective reality, but reality as each side sees it. Differing perceptions often are the major problem in a negotiation. Empathy, or the ability to see the other side's reality, opens the way to solutions. Often, when perceptions are understood even if not agreed to, both sides can offer face-saving concessions. For example, a father who is fearful (perhaps unrealistically) of what he perceives as the loss of his family, may react strongly against the word "visitation" but will accept the same schedule if the language reads "father's time with the children."

Involvement. If a process is to work, all parties must feel that they are participating in that process. Generously giving others credit for ideas creates in their perception a sense of ownership. Often, simply asking the other side to repeat what they have said and writing it down as a good idea can change the dynamics of a negotiation session. If one spouse has sat silently through the preliminary stages of a negotiation, it may be useful for the other sides's attorney to make efforts to draw that spouse into the dialogue: "Joan, you've been listening more intently than we have, can you give us some insight as to why we're stuck on this point?"

Communication. Listening actively to the other side, acknowledging and repeating what has been said and talking directly (not debating) are pivotal. Listening and acknowledging sound simple, but they are difficult skills to develop and crucial to an effective negotiation.

Emotions. They are there and, particularly in a divorce negotiation, they will erupt. Allowing the other side to "let off steam" *without reacting* often clears the air and enables the negotiation to focus on the substantive problems. If the party is letting off steam, be patient. If opposing counsel begins to fume unreasonably, call it. The attorneys are the professionals here and part of their role is to exercise restraint.

Focus on Interests, Not Positions

People's major interests, particularly in a matrimonial context, are security (emotional and economic), sense of belonging, recognition, and control of one's life.

The purpose of the negotiation is to address and resolve those interests within the confines of the situation and practical realities. Priority and individualization of interests for both parties must be clearly and specifically articulated. For example, the attorney might say:

> Bob, we really appreciate your offer to pay the mortgage and taxes directly. But Anne has a need to take control of those pieces of her life now, and the need is an appropriate one. To keep you people financially linked is not what either of you needs. Bob, you have always done all the family finances, and Anne now should and wants to address that in her own right.

Inventing Options For Mutual Gain

There is never one right solution for a problem in the multi-issue area of matrimonial dissolution. Yet experienced practitioners often look at a case and see one right solution with blinding clarity. Such a solution may often be the most efficient and economical but still not be right for this family. Skill at inventing and exploring possible alternatives specific to a particular family is one of the most useful assets of a matrimonial negotiator. Even when working within the strictures of the tax code and with limited assets, a range of variations on standard themes can be explored.

"Negotiation on the merits" works very smoothly if all parties share the values inherent in the process, that is, if the parties to the negotiation (attorneys and clients) use the cooperative style previously defined and are committed to fair resolution.

The process obviously works less smoothly, but does work, when one of the negotiators, either attorney or spouse, is positioned or competitive. The cooperative attorney faced with a competitive negotiator requires concentration and self-control. The major point to bear in mind is not to react to positional tactics and not to get locked into positions. When the opposing side presents a take-it-or-leave-it position, don't accept or reject it but treat it as a possible solution. Ask for advice on options. Continue to ask questions which generate dialogue and allow the other side to get its points across. Use silence creatively. If the other side takes a totally unreasonable position, say nothing. Silence makes people uncomfortable, a nonresponse may create a discomfort that will result in an alternate suggestion or proposal. Threats should be confronted, exposed, and not responded to.

Creativity and inventing options can go only so far in a negotiation. If one is confronted with a four-way negotiating conference in which either opposing counsel or spouse refuses to engage in any give and take, or is acting dishonestly or being abusive, one should stop the conference and leave. Chances are that at the next session (if there is one) the attorney who refused to be abused or to participate in a sham will be accorded more respect.

Experience tells all of us that the bulk of negotiated divorce settlements are finalized in a pressured deadlock atmosphere, often "on the courthouse steps." Because the subject of a divorce agreement has such a long term impact on the parties, their children, and their historical lives, and because the process of negotiating such an agreement can shape the post divorce relationship of the restructured family unit, it behooves matrimonial practitioners to take a hard look at the processes for negotiating they employ to make efforts to use creative strategies for resolving family disputes. The four-way conference is a tool which, when thoughtfully planned and carefully implemented, has extraordinary potential for empowering the divorcing parties to take positive control of their respective new lives.

CHAPTER FIVE
Negotiating a Prenuptial Agreement
Harry M. Fain

Since the passage and recognition of no-fault divorce, the law has made major efforts to minimize the continuing, difficult economic consequences of divorce. With inflation and the need to maintain an accustomed standard of living, usually all members of a family suffer greatly when the family breaks up. Millions of American families who go through the trauma and expense of divorce proceedings inevitably learn the hard lesson that two households cannot live as cheaply as one. More often than not, the court, in dividing the community assets and income, finds that it can do no more than divide deficits between available income and needs.

During the past decade, in an effort to correct inequity between spouses, there has been an upheaval in marital property law. Approximately 40 common law jurisdictions have enacted some form of property division, usually called "equitable distribution" as a principal means of resolving economic dilemmas of property division on dissolution. If one adds the eight community property jurisdictions in which a theoretically equal division of marital property is an inherent aspect of spousal property rights, we can aprpeciate the importance and need for the increasingly utilized prenuptial agreement as a means to clarify and simplify marital rights and obligations.

WHY A PRENUPTIAL AGREEMENT

The prenuptial agreement used to be considered a luxury for the very wealthy, or as one journalist has stated "the nobly born." Today, more and more couples appear to believe that a prenuptial agreement can prevent disputes within the marriage and the acrimony that attends divorce proceedings if the marriage should end. One may properly ask: Why should two people who have known, loved, and trusted each other sufficiently to seek marriage need a prenuptial agreement? One reason is that such agreements clarify what romantic emotion may have left unaddressed. Negotiation of the agreement often identifies the points of disagreement or causes of future disharmony before they reach crisis proportions. In fact, a prenuptial agreement may improve marriage stability and harmony.

The people most likely to negotiate a prenuptial agreement are those who have been married before without one and have suffered or have been "burned" by the economic consequences of divorce proceedings. Since most agreements focus on the property issues, with the complications that develop over characterization and value of property subject to division and disposition, spouses who were unprepared for the consequences of their first divorce proceedings generally want protection, clarity, and a basis for solution if the second marriage should go the way of the first. The new couple may have support obligations to children or former spouses, or may want to protect their children's inheritance claims. Often, a substantial part of the estates of the marrying spouses has been acquired after years of effort, and the spouses do not want the continuity of their effort to be disturbed by claims asserted as a divorce proceeding. Marriages may be threatened or delayed if prenuptial agreements are sought and not concluded.

While each case will vary, based upon the circumstances and expectations of the parties, generally the parties to an agreement hope:

- To avoid the costly, time-consuming, emotional trauma of divorce litigation over property rights and rights to alimony, maintenance, or spousal support.
- To protect the income and assets acquired before and during the marriage.
- To determine clearly economic rights and obligations after marriage including rights of inheritance, and to protect pre-existing assets from estate claims of a spouse.
- To protect established family businesses, professional practices, and pension or retirement rights.
- To assure fair and equal treatment of children from previous marriages and former spouses.
- To provide, if possible, for maintenance or support in the event of divorce, rights that until recently have been zealously guarded as inherently within the jurisdiction of a court to determine.
- To sanction agreements regarding religious upbringing of children. Increasingly, such agreements are being sought. If courts will enforce them despite constitutional objections based on separation of church and state, they may be a valuable safeguard in a society that is witnessing more and more interfaith marriages.

CONDITIONS FOR PRENUPTIAL AGREEMENTS

Because enforcement of a prenuptial agreement invariably involves a determination of its validity in light of precedents litigated over the years, the following questions should be asked by the negotiating parties and their attorneys:

- Was each party fully informed about that party's marital property and economic rights?

- Did each party fully disclose assets and income? Financial statements or balance sheets, reflecting assets and liabilities and disclosing current income, should be exchanged.
- Did each party understand and affirm his or her understanding of the provisions? The attorney would be well-advised to get each page or significant provision of the agreement initialed, to evidence that the parties have read and understood the agreement.
- Was each party represented by independent counsel of his or her choice, without conflict of interest by reason of any prior representation of one of the spouses?
- Was the agreement entered into voluntarily—without duress, undue influence, or unreasonable persuasion?
- Is the agreement fair and reasonable? Does the agreement reflect the parties' complete understanding, with no possible claim that either party may have made representations to the other independently of the agreement?

The foregoing list of concerns is not exclusive. As one writer has characterized such agreements, "They are not cast in stone." If they are challenged, invariably they are subject to the review of judges who sit as courts of equity and who will often be tempted to prevent harsh, inequitable results. Courts will naturally tend to sympathize with the economically weaker party and to intervene in that party's behalf.

SUGGESTED METHODS OF NEGOTIATING

Assume for purposes of discussion that you represent a prospective wife who has limited property and income and minimal prospect of achieving any substantial role in the economic world; she will be essentially a homemaker, wife, and mother. Assume further, for purposes of discussion, that the prospective husband is a successful businessman or professional whose earnings as a result of his talents, efforts, and work will probably enable him to earn substantial amounts of money and increase the value of his existing separate estate during marriage. The proposed agreement contemplates that the wife release or waive her right to inherit, regardless of future circumstances and regardless of the duration of the marriage participation of the wife in the acquisition of income or estate controlled by the husband. Likewise, the prospective husband seeks to retain as separate property his earnings and the appreciated value of separate property derived from his earnings or effort.

In negotiating a prenuptial agreement in such circumstances, questions of fairness and reasonableness should be considered, including the following:

- Assuming the parties are married and not separated, should there not be a right on the part of the wife to inherit or succceed to the marital residence she is occupying, in the event of the death of her husband? If not, should there be a designated period of probate homestead?

- Should a wife be entitled to inherit from the estate of her husband? If so, to what extent and under what circumstances?

- Should there not be consideration for provision of reasonable life insurance in the event of the husband predeceasing the wife?

- In the absence of substantial gifts or estate planning, should there not be guaranteed provision for a source of continued income in the event of the husband's death, either by outright provision in the will or by a trust provided by the husband before the wife gives up the right of probate homestead or family allowance?

- If the husband's anticipated income and profits from his earnings and efforts will be substantial, and if the wife does not participate in those, should there not be provision for annual gifts of liquid assets (which are tax free) but which, on the basis of annual giving, may provide her with a measure of economic independence or security?

- In the alternative, the agreement may give the wife the right to claim marital property and rights of inheritance, based on the length and duration of the marriage. For example, suppose that during the first three to five years of marriage the husband retains exclusive control of his earnings and effort, which are conceded as separate property. If the marriage has survived, should there not be provision for the vesting of rights in the wife, representing marital property for purposes of division as community property, or subject to equitable distribution in a state that provides for such right?

- In situations where the economically superior spouse owns substantial liquid assets, may cash gifts—or transfer of substantially valued liquid assets in the form of securities or bonds as part of an intervivos trust or as outright gift—be available to the wife as her separate property at specified intervals during marriage?

These and other features of a carefully planned agreement can help establish fairness and reasonableness, and therefore enforceability.

WAIVER OF SUPPORT: ENFORCEABILITY

Traditionally, the main purpose of premarital agreements has been to regulate property rights between parties contemplating marriage, in the event of death or divorce. Most jurisdictions have recognized the validity and enforceability of such agreements. As long as the agreements are obtained without fraud or overreaching and reflect full disclosure between the parties of their respective assets, they have generally been upheld.

Historically, agreements that tended to encourage or facilitate divorce were held to be void as against public policy because the state was deemed to have an interest in every marriage. More recently, with the enactment of no-fault legislation, irreconcilable differences form the basis for decreeing a dissolution. The state does not now have the same direct, important interest to preserve a marriage, if the parties by their own action, with or without fault, can decide to dissolve it.

ANTENUPTIAL AGREEMENTS

Under these circumstances, the question has often arisen whether provisions in a prenuptial agreement can be negotiated to provide a predetermined formula for the payment of alimony or spousal support based on such factors as length of marriage, gross and net income, and employability. And can such rights be waived or released by an agreed lump sum payment in the event of divorce?

In 1970, the Florida case of *Posner v. Posner*[1] upheld a prenuptial agreement which provided that $600 per month would be paid to the wife in the event of divorce, as long as there was:

- A fair and equitable provision for the spouse;
- A full disclosure to the prospective spouse of the other spouse's worth; or
- General knowledge of the prospective spouse of the other spouse's worth.

The court addressed the question whether the right to alimony, maintenance, or spousal support could be waived or adjusted by such a contract. The court said:

> We have given careful consideration to the question of whether the change in public policy toward divorce requires a change in the rule respecting Antenuptial Agreements, settling alimony and the property rights of the parties upon divorce and have concluded that such Agreement should no longer be held to be void ab initio as "contrary to public policy."

The court held that alimony provisions were enforceable as long as the premarital agreement was free from fraud, mistake, duress, misrepresentation, or nondisclosure; was not unconscionable; and was not unfair and unreasonable at the time of judgment due to changed facts and circumstances.

Other cases have since dealt with the same issue, and have

---

[1] 233 So.2d 381 (Fla. 1970).

indicated a willingness to enforce prenuptial agreements affecting the right of support or maintenance.[2] In *Newman v. Newman* the Supreme Court of Colorado said:

> We hold that, even though an Antenuptial Agreement is entered into in good faith, with full disclosure and without any element or fraud or over reaching, the maintenance provisions thereof may become voidable for unconscionability occasioned by circumstances existing at the time of marriage dissolution.[3]

Thus, one can reasonably expect judicial review of a waiver of maintenance or alimony at the time the marriage is dissolved. The essential question remains: What constitutes an unconscionable waiver of alimony, maintenance, or spousal support? The language of the Uniform Marriage and Divorce Act, in its maintenance section,[4] provides that the court can grant a maintenance order for either spouse, in spite of such a provision and in spite of waiver, only if it finds that the spouse seeking it:

- Lacks sufficient property, including marital property apportioned to him or her, to provide for his or her reasonable needs; and
- Is unable to support himself or herself through appropriate employment, or is the custodian of a child whose condition or circumstances make it appropriate that the custodian not be required to seek employment outside of the home.

Thus, a spouse who claims that a premarital agreement is unconscionable because of a waiver of maintenance or alimony must prove that, at the time of the divorce, the agreement rendered him or her without means of reasonable support.

---

[2]In particular *see*, Newman v. Newman, 653 P.2d 728 (Colo. 1982); Osborne v. Osborne, 384 Mass. 591, 428 N.E.2d 810 (1981); Unander v. Unander, 265 Or. 102, 506 P.2d 719 (1973); Volid v. Volid, 6 Ill.App.3d 386, 286 N.E.2d 42 (1972).

[3]653 P.2d 728, 734 (1982).

[4]Section 308(a) (2) (1974).

It follows that if a spouse seeks to predetermine a formula for the alimony, support, or maintenance provisions in event of divorce, fairness and reasonableness should be demonstrated to avoid the consequence of a court's disapproval of such cause for unconscionability.

CONCLUSION

To negotiate a prenuptial agreement requires not only knowledge of substantive law and understanding of the objectives to be achieved, but also a well-developed style of negotiation.

Lawyers should strive to find terms upon which the parties can agree, and set them accurately in writing. It might be preferable to attempt to reach agreement on a few matters with certainty, rather than on many matters in general terms that are later attacked or bring about marital disharmony.

A lawyer should not advise a client to agree to any term that the client does not intend to honor. Equally, it may be counterproductive to advise a client to insist on a term or provision to which the other party is known to be hostile, unless the client has been advised that he or she may risk the marriage in insisting upon the provision. In such circumstances, depending upon the pressures of time and arrangements for the wedding, the attorney's best procedure may be to tell his client that a particular term or even the entire contract cannot be effectively negotiated.

Above all, as a protection against a later charge of undue influence or fraud, the prospective bride or groom should be warned by his or her attorney that threats to call off the marriage (after the marriage has been fully planned) may constitute coercion, and thereafter the premarital agreement may be subject to attack by reason of coercion or pressure.

In the last analysis, the prenuptial agreement should be structured so that the final product will be one that supports marriage, including recognition that it is a binding agreement with respect to the existing property rights of each party and future acquisitions of property. This may mean giving up certain rights, but on the other hand may gain other concessions. If entered into with knowledge and understanding the agreement can have the best possible results.

In an authoritative expression of judicial attitudes toward prenuptial agreements, the California Supreme Court in the case of *In re Marriage of Dawley*,[5] stated the following:

> In times past antenuptial agreements were most often used by wealthy men and women who feared that less wealthy finances might be marrying for money. In recent years, however, an increasing number of couples have executed antenuptial agreements in order to structure their legal relationship in a manner more suited to their needs and values.... Neither the reordering of property rights to fit the needs and desires of the couple, nor realistic planning that takes account of the possibility of dissolution, offends the public policy favoring and protecting marriage. It is only when the terms of an agreement go further—when they promote and encourage dissolution, and thereby threaten to induce the destruction of a marriage that might otherwise endure—that such terms offend public policy.
>
> For the reasons we have explained, the agreement at bar does not fall within this ban. Having freely contracted that the earnings of each, and property derived from those earnings, will be the separate property of the earning spouse, the parties are bound by their agreement.

It is safe to predict that prenuptial agreements will be increasingly utilized in today's unpredictable marital climate. Family law practitioners must acquire the knowledge and skills needed to meet the challenge and responsibility of negotiating prenuptial agreements that support and strengthen marriage but minimize or reduce conflict and unfortunate consequences if the marriage should dissolve.

---

[5] 17 Cal.3d 342, 358, 551 P.2d 323, 333, 131 Cal.Rptr. 3, 13 (1976).

CHAPTER SIX
The Settlement Process— the View From the Bench*
Edward M. Ginsburg

Because most divorce matters are rarely tried to judgment but are settled either before trial or during the proceedings, the real question is when and under what circumstances settlement is reached. In response to public complaints that the process takes too long, costs too much, and is never over, judges and lawyers alike must take responsibility for making a traumatic experience as painless and constructive as possible.

The burgeoning new industry promoting alternatives to the traditional method of resolving disputes is testimony to the extent of the dissatisfaction with the current system. Although more than 92 percent of all cases, including divorce matters, are resolved short of trial, the public perceives the judicial system as promoting conflict rather than fostering constructive settlement. Lawyers and judges must work together to improve both the perception and performance of the current system. Failure to do so could result in total rejection of the process developed over time to carefully protect the rights of the public, in favor of panaceas that will serve neither the long-term interests of the bench and bar nor the public welfare.

---

*The author wishes to thank Butterworth Legal Publishers for permission to reprint this article, which appeared in slightly different form in the Massachusetts Family Law Journal (March 1985).

As a judge who has participated in and observed the process for a number of years, I would like to point out several factors that are particularly important in determining when and under what circumstances family law concerns are resolved. First, time is never neutral. The busy lawyer who reacts to the pressures of the moment feels a great temptation to postpone or continue a matter less pressing to the lawyer than to the client. Sometimes it is a client who seeks the delay, who wants to put off the day of reckoning or frustrate the other side. Particularly when young children are involved, time is very significant. A child perceives time differently than an adult does. From Christmas to Christmas for a 50-year-old man is nothing, for a three-year-old child, an eternity. For a grandparent, driving several hours to see a grandchild may be a nice ride in the country. For the grandchild, making the same trip is a different story. We must be more sensitive to the impact of time, and particularly the impact of delay on the parties going through the divorce process.

Another important task is the setting of realistic expectations. Parties look to the divorce process to meet needs that the system cannot meet. For lawyers to encourage or allow their clients the luxury of believing that the court system or any other form of dispute negotiation can cure their emotional hurts, reward their virtues, and punish their spouse's shortcomings is a disservice to the system and to the public. When the client is finally forced to face the reality that, in most cases, the court system or any other system can only make an equitable division of an inadequate amount of money and establish time-sharing arrangements with minor children in the post-divorce family, the unrealistic expectations give way to despair and disillusionment. How much more professional it is for the lawyer to tell the client from the beginning what the system can and cannot accomplish, and to help the client adjust to realistic expectations for settlement.

There are two basic reasons why most cases settle short of a complete trial. In all cases, whether or not the parties will have an ongoing relationship after the trial, the parties who go to trial run the risk of an unpredictable result at best and a loss at worst. Faced with these alternatives, parties in most situations call for a compromise rather than a spin of the roulette wheel. Thus, the person involved in an automobile accident would rather settle for a smaller monetary award (compared to a potential verdict) than run the risk of getting nothing.

In cases in which the parties will have to cooperate with each other after the resolution of the immediate dispute, such as divorce cases, there is an added incentive for settlement. Bloodletting, in which one partner accuses the other of all sorts of indiscretions in order to gain a monetary advantage in a property division, is not conducive to fostering cooperation for the sake of the minor children in the restructured family after the divorce. In addition, when parties participate in the formulation of their own agreement, the evidence is overwhelming that they are more likely to live by it and avoid multiple court appearances than when the arrangements have been imposed on them by a court judgment.

The prerequisite of any rational settlement is getting the parties together and providing them with sufficient information for realistic settlement negotiations. If the parties are to engage in meaningful discussions, cat and mouse games must be discouraged. By the same token, abuses of discovery procedures in which the deep pocket wears out the weaker side must be avoided. The role of the court in fostering settlement is to see that all relevant information is produced but that unnecessary and oppressive discovery is avoided.

The most efficient means for the judge to get the parties together for meaningful discussion with adequate information is through the use of a uniformly enforced pretrial order. To be effective the pretrial order must unequivocally require two elements: the exchange of complete and accurate information between the parties; and the requirement that the parties and counsel meet in person after receiving the order and before preparing the pretrial memorandum for the scheduled court conference.

If the parties have not had a meaningful exchange of information and have neither agreed upon the essential issues nor delineated where the disagreements lie, they will be unable to resolve the problems themselves. And the court will be in no position to offer constructive assistance. For example, if the central issue is the equitable division of the marital assets, and the parties arrive at a pretrial conference with only rough "guesstimates" of the values of the assets, they are not in a position to get much help from the court. If, on the other hand, the parties have stipulated the values of the assets or have obtained dependable independent appraisals, the court can help resolve the conflict between them.

The in-person meeting between counsel and parties before coming to court is crucial. Although counsel will often claim that they have discussed the issues by telephone, or that the parties are so hostile to each other that a meeting would be counterproductive, that ultimate decision is not for counsel or parties to make. To have the first meaningful, face-to-face negotiations in the courthouse corridor is not conducive to rational settlement. The atmosphere in which the parties are brought together is very important. The hurly-burly of a congested courthouse corridor does not provide an atmosphere for calm negotiations. A conference room with a round table and soft lighting makes a significant difference in the negotiation process. Although the judge has little control over the facilities in the courthouse, lawyers at the meeting before the pretrial conference can select a setting that will facilitate negotiations.

My experience is that in 95 percent of those cases in which counsel insist that a meeting in person between clients and counsel will at best accomplish nothing and at worst exacerbate the situation, they have misjudged the human dynamics. This court-mandated meeting is almost always productive. In a large percentage of cases, parties and counsel faced with the hard work of preparing for the pretrial conference come to grips with the issues and settle the case. Rather than expending additional time and money in preparing for battle, they realistically assess their positions and work out a compromise.

Parties who either have not spoken to each other in many months or perhaps have never met in person have the opportunity to communicate directly with one another rather than receive second-hand information from their lawyers. This form of hearsay can easily lead to misunderstanding and later to distrust of the legal process. How often litigants report that they feel that the case had gotten totally out of their control and, guided by lawyers, assumed a life of its own! The mandatory meeting affords to the parties the opportunity to have input into the resolution process. Even when the parties cannot reach complete accord, they can often sufficiently narrow the issues so that counsel and the judge can help them resolve the case at the pretrial conference.

In brief, the mandatory in-person meeting between parties and counsel prior to the pretrial conference should never be waivable by counsel and should be waived by the court after written motion only in the most compelling circumstances.

The time for the pretrial conference should be fixed in the pretrial order sufficiently in advance so that parties and counsel have the opportunity to complete discovery, hold the in-person meeting, and prepare the pretrial memorandum that outlines all the issues, lists the witnesses to be called, and premarks all exhibits. A pretrial conference is very different from a status conference. At a status conference the participants must merely ascertain what has to be done to ready the case for trial; at a pretrial conference, however, parties and counsel should be prepared for trial. By the time of the latter conference, all discovery should be complete, leaving counsel, the parties, and the judge in a position to assess the case realistically.

Once the date of the pretrial conference is set, it should not be continued except for compelling reasons. If counsel have conflicts, the court should be informed as soon as possible. If the pretrial conference date is fixed several weeks ahead, and counsel seek a continuance a few days before the scheduled date in order to complete discovery or meet another engagement that was known well in advance or that came up after the notice of the pretrial conference date, the judge should be very wary of granting a continuance. The reason given for the requested continuance is in too many instances a coverup either for counsel's inexcusable neglect in failing to carry out the requirements of the pretrial order or for the parties' desire to delay the proceedings. Once counsel and parties learn that the court date is firm, the system will function much more efficiently and fairly. Counsel and parties should have the right to expect the court to be ready to serve them and, by the same token, be ready to give the court the opportunity to be of service.

A strictly enforced pretrial order is a very successful vehicle in and of itself for promoting the settlement of cases. What other role can a judge play in the settlement process? Some judges, particularly in jury-waived cases over which they will preside, feel uncomfortable making recommendations for possible settlement. Other judges do not hesitate to make recommendations based on the written materials presented at the pretrial conference.

Quite often counsel will agree on the contours of what they believe to be a fair settlement, but one or both may be having difficulties dealing with the client. Counsel look to the judge as an authority to help control clients' unrealistic expectations. Under such circumstances, judges should have few qualms about venturing a recommendation. If counsel agree on the settlement value of the case and their recommendation falls within the normal guidelines for such cases, the court should have little difficulty helping them deal with the unrealistic expectations of an unreasonable client. The mere statement by the court that the proposed settlement seems reasonable is often enough to resolve the case.

When parties and counsel differ over the language or form of a settlement, as opposed to the substance, a judge is often in a position to promote settlement by suggesting cosmetic changes acceptable to everyone. For example, although the parties may have worked out the substance of the custodial relationship, the mother may insist on the label "sole legal custody" and the father may be equally adamant in calling the relationship "joint legal custody." Both parties, at the suggestion of the court, might accept the label "shared legal custody."

Another category of dispute concerns those cases in which the parties agree on the basic facts but not on the conclusion to be drawn from those facts. This may occur, for example, when the "marital assets" consists of property derived from many sources, including gifts and inheritance, and the lawyers are looking for some indication of the manner in which the court will treat the inherited property in making an equitable division. Counsel often look to the court for guidance when the basic fact pattern is undisputed. As long as the judge makes it clear that his or her opinion is based on the facts as then agreed upon and reserves the right to change that opinion if the evidence turns out differently at trial, the judge is not vulnerable to criticism for prejudging the case.

A more difficult situation arises when counsel cannot agree on the facts. These cases fall into two categories. Sometimes the facts that excite the parties are not relevant to the dispute. The parties may be fighting about their relative conduct during the marriage. The issue for the court to decide is their respective contributions towards child support, which depends upon their relative incomes. The incomes are not a matter in dispute. Under these circumstances, the court should feel free to help the parties separate the relevant from the irrelevant considerations and make a recommendation based on the former.

More difficult is the case in which material facts are in dispute. In such a case, the court must be careful to condition all recommendations with the qualification that if the evidence turns out at trial to be different from what appears at the pretrial conference, the ultimate decision may be different from the recommendation. In fact, the evidence often does turn out to be different at trial, where the demeanor of the witnesses plays an important role.

The court can tell the parties that this conference gives them the opportunity to resolve their own case. The court can remind the parties that no one willingly surrenders his or her fate to an outsider, that only they know the real situation, that it is more prudent for them to resolve the matter than to risk the vagaries and added expense of a trial. Quite often the parties have not considered the additional expense of protracted litigation and reach the conclusion that the differences separating them are not worth the additional cost and risk of the fight. The court has not unduly prejudged a situation by pointing out these important considerations.

Finally, judges and lawyers should recognize those categories of cases in which settlement negotiations are futile. No one should waste time trying to settle those few cases in which the difference between the parties is too wide to bridge: for example, if the parties' perceptions of the facts are so different that they are not really talking about the same case, or if the parties are hung up over matters of principle and insist upon using the court as a forum for vindication. The most subtle form of case not susceptible to settlement involves the so-called "hostility junkie." On the surface the "hostility junkie" often appears to be quite reasonable. His or her position is close to that of the other side, but he or she can never reach closure. Wittingly or unwittingly, this person misuses the settlement process to prolong the litigation. Once any of these situations is recognized, the judge should pace the case on the trial list without wasting further time in settlement negotiations.

The time between the pretrial conference and the trial date is most significant. In order to force the parties realistically to come to terms with the issues in the case at the pretrial conference, it is imperative that the scheduled trial date be imminent. If counsel and parties feel that the trial date is far off, the natural tendency toward procrastination will interfere with the necessity to face the situation. In addition, one of the parties might be tempted to use the pretrial process as a means of testing the other side without engaging in good-faith bargaining. If the trial is imminent, both the tendency to procrastinate and the temptation to misuse the process are minimized.

If the parties arrive at a settlement at the pretrial conference, the agreement should be reduced to writing immediately. The situations are legion, particularly in highly charged domestic relations cases, in which the parties announce a settlement in court and then several days later report that the agreement came apart in the drafting process. To avoid the problem of second thoughts or bickering over terms, the essentials of the agreement should be reduced to writing at the time of settlement. If necessary, the parties can be given additional time to file a more formal typed agreement, which can be substituted for the original agreement. The court should make it clear, however, that if the parties end up arguing over the terms of the more formal agreement, the original agreement as filed will be binding.

THE SETTLEMENT PROCESS

Recognition of effective settlement techniques is an integral part of the trial process. Before a case is entered in court, counsel and parties determine the pace of negotiations. Once a case is docketed, the court assumes an obligation to make the settlement process as fair and expeditious as possible. By setting and adhering to meaningful pretrial procedures, lawyers and judges can work together to promote the settlement of cases quickly and under circumstances designed to minimize pain for the parties. For those few cases that cannot be settled, the court system affords safeguards to ensure a degree of fairness that no alternative dispute resolution can provide.

CHAPTER SEVEN
Negotiating Under the Demand of the Judge

Martin L. Aronson

In addition to the basic principles involved in negotiating the settlement of a matrimonial case, there are special factors that may apply when we are negotiating under the demand of a judge. I offer the following thoughts and ideas to be considered by counsel when attempting to settle a divorce case under the immediate control of the court.

Know all the facts. It is hazardous and foolhardy to appear before the court without complete knowledge of all the evidence you will use to prove the substantive grounds and the financial posture of both parties. You will be at a decided disadvantage if you attempt to negotiate settlement, particularly in the presence of the judge, without complete and fluent familiarity with all the facts. If you are fully prepared, you will impress the court; if you are not, you will do your client a disservice.

Be prepared for trial. At a pretrial conference or other negotiating session in the presence of the court, the case should be fully prepared for trial. If you have done all that is necessary in preparing your party, witnesses, and evidence, you will be able to negotiate from strength. If you are not fully prepared, the judge will be less impressed with the representations you make, and your client will suffer the consequences. It is dangerous to attempt to settle a case at court simply because you are not prepared to try the case within the ensuing days or weeks.

Settlement authority. Do not attempt to negotiate a settlement under the demand of the judge unless you have full authority from your client to do so.

Time and place to negotiate. A cantankerous and litigious lawyer may decline to enter into meaningful negotiations prior to a court appearance. He seems to have some need for the presence of a judge to compel settlement talks. Unfortunately, all too many lawyers proceed on the theory that they are going to achieve maximum results only when they have all parties in court reacting to the judge's recommendations. Depending upon the nature of your client and of your adversary, the facts of the case, and the philosophies of the judge, this can be an effective method *on occasion*; however, it is foolhardy to develop such a practice on a regular basis. You will quickly earn the reputation of one who puts on the war paint but drops the bow and arrow in the courtroom—afraid to negotiate without the judge, and afraid to try the case if a satisfactory settlement cannot be achieved.

It is, of course, essential always to be mindful that you are involved in an adversarial process. However, your approach should be one of professional cooperation whenever possible, and this should begin long before you reach the courthouse steps. Establishing a good rapport with your adversary will often lead to more meaningful negotiations both prior to reaching the courthouse and while under the demand of the judge. Furthermore, a judge will appreciate the effort made by the lawyers to reach a settlement acceptable to both parties. Of course, a cooperative atmosphere is not always possible. In those cases the appropriate time and place in which to negotiate is before the court.

Communicate with your client. If you are going to adopt the position of "using the court" to initiate and guide settlement, then you must be certain to so advise your client. Once a lawyer tells his client, "We are going to court . . . we are going to trial," the client will justifiably take that quite literally and may be distraught, confused, and unreasonable during sudden efforts to settle the dispute at court. It is a basic necessity, therefore, to keep your client informed of all substantive happenings in the case and to share with him or her your planned tactics for settlement. He should be prepared so that he is not surprised at the flavor of courthouse settlement efforts.

Remember that your client is unfamiliar with the litigation process. Because of the emotions involved in a divorce, it is not uncommon for a client to lose his sense of reasonableness or to be overwhelmed by confusion. Your communication with your client is essential to avoid the clouding or distortion of thought that may result in an unfair resolution or in unwise concessions that might not have been made if your client had a better understanding of the situation.

Explain the judge's idiosyncrasies in detail to your client. This will be helpful both for the actual trial of the case and for understanding suggestions the court may make with respect to settlement.

Dealing with the judge. If efforts to settle the case outside the court have failed, we must factor in the judge's approach and settlement philosophy. In addition to mastering the facts of our own case, learning enough about our client so that we may maintain appropriate influence and control during negotiations, and knowing our adversary's case, we must learn about the likes and dislikes of the assigned judge regarding settlement:

- Does the judge participate actively in efforts to settle or display an indifferent, passive attitude? Does he tend to become significantly involved in the unresolved issues, probe the differences, and make specific recommendations, or is his style more perfunctory: Will he simply suggest that counsel step outside and see if they can work things out?

- How detailed will the judge be in examining financial statements prior to becoming involved in negotations? Is it her custom to be somewhat superficial regarding content until trial, or does she delve into the financial statement and use it in directing discussions about the parties financial positions?

- How much does the judge pay attention to the grounds for divorce? Most judges will not want to hear a great deal of discussion of whether a husband or wife was "sleeping around," or "who screamed at whom in front of the kids." They will not want the conference to bog down in dirty laundry. If the parties agree that a divorce should be granted but differ over monetary matters, the judge is more apt to play an active role in helping to resolve the financial differences.

If your jurisidiction has a statute similar to Massachusetts,[1] listing the conduct of the parties as one of the factors the court may or shall consider in distributing assets, and if you have substantial evidence regarding the other side's negative conduct, what course should you follow during negotiations? Suggestion: Make every effort to highlight that evidence succinctly. (Be diplomatic. You don't want to irritate the judge whose general disposition is not to hear such matters in chambers.) Emphasize that only because the evidence is blatant and because of the conduct statute do you bring such matters to the fore. If you are in conference with a judge whose practice is more liberal regarding discussion of grounds, then, of course, act accordingly.

- Should we have meaningful settlement conferences with the judge who is going to hear the case? There is always a possibility that a judge may be prejudiced by what has come out during negotiation efforts, but such a result is rare. Most judges who involve themselves in assisting counsel to settle are quite capable of maintaining objectivity and putting aside during trial whatever settlement discussions took place in their presence. The inexperienced lawyer, who is apt to be cynical about the court's ability to do this, should learn quickly that most judges do master

---

[1] Mass. Gen. L. Ch. 208, ¶334 (1984).

the ability. Certainly, judges are human and are bound to be influenced to some extent by pretrial remarks or data, but by and large it is my experience that judges make every effort to base their decisions upon evidence, not upon pretrial talk.

- We have all been faced with that case in which pretrial conference with the court results in a perfectly sound and reasonable proposal, but our client's obstinancy, vindictiveness, distrust, or lack of reason results in a refusal to accept the proposal. A judge may believe such an attitude is reprehensible and obstructionist. He may be right. But if your client insists upon going forward with trial after you have thoroughly explained all reasons why the suggested solution is sound, then you must *consider* moving that the judge recuse herself. If done diplomatically, you will not endanger your future relationship with the judge.

- Must a written agreement be completed and executed at court? If you reach an accord, is it the judge's practice to keep the parties at court until a written agreement is signed? Judges vary in this regard. It may be that because of the history of the case, the personalities of the parties, or your belief that you got an extraordinary deal, it will be to your advantage to keep the parties at the courthouse until they execute an agreement. If the judge has not directed this course of action, suggest it to the court. If the settlement is fair, it is important to avoid the danger that the parties will change their minds.

- However, you must also give consideration to other factors which weigh against preparing and executing the agreement in court. You do not want your client to feel that he or she was pressured into signing an agreement; you want to be sure that the client understands all the terms and has had an opportunity to think about and digest the resolution. If most of the issues were settled prior to coming under the judge's "gun," and the remaining few matters were then resolved at the courthouse, this may be an ideal case in which to complete the agreement at court. If you doubt your client's full understanding of the ramifications of the proposal, impress this upon the court, request an order that the parties return on a specific date with an agreement or be ready for trial. Don't leave completion of the agreement open-ended; it may drift and the parties may retreat from what you consider a good result.

Also, in writing an agreement at the courthouse, you may omit some provisions that may not be paramount but would ordinarily have been included had you been given the opportunity to prepare the agreement in your office. "Think time" is important to everyone. Having to prepare an agreement at the courthouse immediately after exhausting settlement talks can result in sloppy draftsmanship and error.

Generally, unless you fear the loss of a good settlement you should request whatever reasonable time you can obtain from the court to return with an agreement. Put the request on the record. If the court does not do so on its own, ask for an order.

- Some judges lean too heavily in directing that a case be settled—their basic approach is that every domestic relations case can be settled. They participate forcefully and apply a great deal of pressure to have the parties resolve their differences through the negotiation process. Their motives are good but in some cases misdirected. One technique is to assign a case for a pretrial conference, and if the parties fail to settle at the conference, order the case to trial that day. Although one may argue that this is unfair, that the court should simply assign the case for trial with the understanding that a conference will precede the trial, it is a technique that some judges contend results in settlement. The parties are not psychologically geared for trial when the assignment is for a pretrial conference. The sudden directive that the case proceed may cause a sudden reversal and result in a settlement. But does it result in a fair settlement?

An ancient technique is to call the case for trial (together with other cases), not clearly informing counsel of the actual likelihood of getting started that day, and keeping the parties in the courthouse for the day in hope of bringing them together. On occasion this methods works. But be careful. Do we settle cases under this kind of pressure (hanging around the courthouse corridor for a day becomes a month) for less or do we give away more than what is fair and reasonable?

We are advocates first. We must do whatever is appropriate in our client's best interest. When the court brings undue pressure, we must always remember that we have lived with our case and that we are far more knowledgeable of the facts, the subtleties, and the client's needs than is the judge. Be pleasantly firm in guarding your position. Do not resist the court's efforts to have you negotiate—even if you believe the case cannot be settled. Be circumspect. If the judge inquires whether you have made an effort to settle the case, respond candidly and indicate to the court your willingness to make further attempts to negotiate. In some situations you are better advised to appease the court (again, assuming that you are before a judge who leans heavily toward encouraging settlement) and indicate your willingness to sit and talk with your adversary despite the reality that to do so will be mere game-playing. When you return to the judge and inform him that efforts to settle have failed, be diplomatic and be firm (not stubborn) in holding onto your bottom-line position regarding the unresolved issues.

CHAPTER EIGHT
The Dynamics of Mediation
W. Patrick Phear

Much has been written and even more spoken about the growing practice of resolving family disputes, particularly divorce-related disputes, with the help of a mediator. Since Coogler's[1] initial description of a highly structured divorce mediation process, the literature has been progressively from promoting the use of mediation[2] to describing its actual process and intricacies.[3,4] The recent national consensus on standards of practice[5,6] reflects a general acceptance of a mediation model[7] that would be familiar to labor mediators and volunteers in numerous community mediation programs across the United States.

---

[1] O.J. Coogler, STRUCTURED MEDIATION IN DIVORCE SETTLEMENTS (1978).
[2] R. Coulson, FIGHTING FAIR (1983).
[3] J. Folberg & A. Taylor, MEDIATION (1984).
[4] C. W. Moore, THE MEDIATION PROCESS (1986).
[5] STANDARDS OF PRACTICE FOR LAWYER MEDIATORS IN FAMILY DISPUTES ((1984).
[6] MODEL STANDARDS OF PRACTICE: FAMILY AND DIVORCE MEDIATION (Ass'n. of Family and Conciliation Courts Symposia, 1984).
[7] Phear, *Divorce Mediation: The Parameters of Practice are Shaped by a Consensus of Standards*, 2 MASS. FAM. L. J. 84, 84–86 (1985).

Mediation in its most generally accepted form is a process in which a trained neutral third party helps the disputing parties come to a mutually satisfactory resolution of their own design. The mediator has no coercive powers and cannot bind the parties either to continue to try to mediate their differences or to accept a particular outcome. In any mediation the first order of business is to clarify what the scope of the mediation will be and what items are on the bargaining table. In some cases there are issues that would be better resolved in a different forum, issues that are primarily psychological or that involve areas of substantive law. These issues need to be screened out of the mediation effort or resolved beforehand. The parties are then asked to commit themselves to negotiating with each other in good faith and agreeing to full disclosure of all relevant facts and information in order to ensure that any final agreement is indeed fair.

While not all court-based mediation models allow both the parties and the mediator to respect fully the confidentiality of all communications and work product made or derived during mediation, such confidentiality is thought by many[8] to be a crucial ingredient for a successful and enduring outcome. Some states, like Massachusetts, have ensured this confidentiality by statute; other states, like Connecticut, have done so by court rule. In any event it is essential that the mediator specifically address the subject of confidentiality and let the family know the circumstances under which the mediator would not be able to respect their confidences.

Current Standards of Practice expressly prohibit the mediator's offering advice to the parties, limiting his or her role to providing needed information when the mediator does possess substantive knowledge[9]. This makes it essential that the parties have access to outside advisers wherever their dispute requires partisan advice. The final agreement has to be mutually acceptable to the parties, and in the case of divorcing

---

[8]Folberg, *supra* note 3, at 263–80.
[9]Milne, *Model Standards of Practice for Family and Divorce Mediation*, 8 MEDIATION Q. 78 (1985).

couples, the final agreement will have to be accepted and endorsed by a judge before it can be binding.

The parties are free to abandon the mediation attempt at any time when they feel the process is not meeting their needs, or if they come to believe it unlikely to result in an acceptable product. Most mediators reserve for themselves, too, the right to terminate their involvement in the case should they decide that one or other of the parties is not bargaining in good faith, or is using the process to gain unfair advantage over a spouse who is unable to negotiate for himself or herself. This requires that the whole process, including any free structure, be designed in such a way that either party can indeed withdraw without incurring significant penalties for initially attempting to mediate and then deciding that it would be better not to proceed. In some instances, if there is no blanket confidentiality, a party might be tempted to pretend to try to mediate, perhaps to acquire information that would otherwise be available only through extensive legal discovery motions.

There is no consensus on what constitutes a successful mediation outcome. Court-based mediation programs tend to regard reaching agreement as the sole criterion for success; community programs often consider not only whether an agreement is reached but also how well the agreement meets the participants' complaints, and how well the agreement holds up over time.

There are indeed several levels of success. One level is the parties' agreement, in mediation, on which issues need resolution and on the necessity for cooperative input to achieve resolution. A second success level will be reached if the parties can determine why they have different views and which factors, or hard facts, must be considered as they try for an agreement to meet their joint and separate interests. The third and final success occurs when the parties reach a mutually acceptable and durable agreement, which both endorse and have a long-term investment in living up to, in spirit and letter.

The process itself is most easily discussed and understood by following a composite couple's mediator-assisted separation negotiations. Bob and Sue Salkins had been married 12 years when they finally agreed that their marriage was over. In those years they had had two children, Tom (10) and Gail (8). Nine years ago they had bought a house. Bob was a regional branch manager at a local bank earning close to $40,000 a year; Sue had last worked as a nursery school teacher 10 years ago, before Tom was born. It was Sue who initially decided, after a year of marriage therapy, that she'd had enough. She now wanted Bob to work with her to end their marriage rather than to preserve it, and she wanted him to move out of the house. Bob absolutely refused to move out and was still uncertain whether their marriage was irretrievable. At the end of several weeks of escalating arguments they both consulted lawyers, and after reviewing their options decided to try to resolve their differences through mediation.

Bob Salkins contacted a mediator recommended by his lawyer. After Bob had received a brief explanation of mediation costs and a general description of the process, he agreed to have Sue call and confirm one of the two tentative initial appointments. Sue needed the same information and had questions about the mediator's background, qualifications, and experience[10] before she too agreed to meet for an exploratory session.

Both good mediation practice and current Standards of Practice[11] require that the mediator help the couple consider the advantages and disadvantages of other dispute resolution options. The option chosen will tend to shape not only the outcome of the dispute but also the parties' future relations[12].

---

[10] Most experienced divorce mediators will have had training in conflict resolution and management, mediation theory and practice, the psychological aspects of divorce (parents and children), the legal process and procedures, divorce-related tax law, financial planning, and professional ethics. In addition to this didactic information, a mediator will have had to acquire training and experience in how to appropriately use this information within an acceptable mediation model.

[11] Milne, *supra* note 9, at 75.

[12] J. S. Auerbach, JUSTICE WITHOUT LAW 12 (1983) (quoting Simon, *The Ideology of Advocacy: Procedural Justice and Professional Ethics,* 1978 WIS. L. REV. 29, 115).

In this case, given the Salkins' history and that they had carefully decided on mediation with the advice of their attorneys, this was a relatively brief part of the initial session. Sue was adamant that for her the marriage was over, as was marriage therapy. She was willing to leave open the question of divorce therapy, but saw this as contingent on their actually separating. Bob was equally adamant in his wish to try to reach agreement through mediation prior to asking their lawyers to negotiate with each other on their behalf. A distant, mutually acceptable deadline was set, three months hence, for when the mediation attempt would end.

The discussion about options is important. It minimizes the possibility that couples will attempt to mediate when mediation is inappropriate and when mediation is appropriate it reinforces the parties' commitment to the process. In general, mediation is inappropriate when one of the parties lacks the mental ability to make rational judgments, either because of a mental deficiency, lack of cognitive ability, or mental impairment due to a psychological state or chronic dependence on drugs or alcohol. Serious allegations involving such abuse or dependence, if they are denied by the other party, also make mediation an unacceptable option.

In most divorces both parties are dispute resolution novices and have done very little structured thinking about the pros and cons of the options available to them. It is easy for an inexperienced or unscrupulous mediator to talk the parties into continuing to try to mediate despite factors that make mediation a less than viable option. When mediation is appropriate early, informed commitment is essential to the process. If the family is to reach a fair, reasonable, and mutually acceptable agreement, they will have to spend considerable time working hard, and they might well jeopardize their ability to benefit from one of the other dispute resolution techniques available to them. The agreement will need to be based not only on full financial and personal disclosure in a legal sense, but also on both parties' full understanding of the information and its implications. To reach such an agreement by consensus and without relying on a tie-breaking vote or on the imposed decision of an outside authority takes a strong commitment.

Before proceeding most mediators require the formal commitment of the parties to a serious effort at resolving their differences through mediation. This is usually done after the mediator has obtained a general understanding of the dispute in order to ensure that the mediator has the requisite knowledge, skills, and experience and after it is clear who all the parties are and who will actually be present during the sessions: parents, children, and their crucially important outside advisers (family members, therapists, and lawyers). Bob and Sue signed a formal commitment to try mediation. It specified that:

- They could unilaterally withdraw from the mediation at any time;
- All communications and work product would be confidential in the event that the mediation attempt failed;
- They would not call the mediator as a witness in any subsequent legal action regarding the issues discussed in mediation;
- They both understood that the mediator would not be providing them with advice, and with only limited amounts of information;
- They were both free to seek the counsel of outside professionals.

For a mediator the initial session with a couple is always an interesting and challenging event. This is the mediator's first opportunity to begin to assess the parties' individual and collective strengths and weaknesses and their negotiating style and abilities. In the case of the Salkins, it was soon apparent that Sue had indeed adjusted to the idea that the marriage was over. She was full of enthusiasm and excited about the prospect of being single and not having to be considerate of Bob and his needs. Bob, in stark contrast, appeared downcast, and he fluctuated between trying to regain Sue's approval at almost any cost and stubbornly refusing to acknowledge her point of view.

This combination, not a particularly unusual one, did raise real questions about their ability to represent themselves. Special attention would need to be paid to slowing the mediation process in order to prevent hasty, poorly understood agreements. Bob might well need additional therapeutic help, and Sue might need a lot more objective and dispassionate counsel than she seemed to anticipate. This was not a couple to encourage to settle quickly. Like most couples, they would spend a great deal of effort in the initial session trying to convince the mediator of the correctness of 'their case'. It would take time before they came to believe that it really was they and not the mediator who would resolve their differences.

The initial work of the mediator is to help the parties to truly hear what the other person is saying, and to do this while managing the manifest conflict in a way that is ultimately productive. The mediator has to work actively with the parties. He must help them restate their concerns and hopes in ways that keep a variety of options open. Statements like "I insist on having custody of MY children" have to be broken down and reframed in ways that reflect the constituent pieces: "You are concerned about who will be making decisions on behalf of your children, and you would prefer, if it is to be only one parent, that you both agree that you be this parent." Specific statements must be recast to reflect general areas of concern that will be examined and considered later, once the scope and the implications of all the necessary decisions have been examined and understood.

The parties have a wealth of information that the mediator requires, and they often have a real need to express their feelings, which might or might not be useful in the mediation process. The parties will persist in their natural tendency to try again to resolve their dispute in ways that have worked, or in this case not worked, in the past, and to view the mediator as someone to convince of the correctness of their view. It is essential that the mediator take charge, and work to balance both the intensity of the communications and the amount of air time each party has. This must be done purposefully and carefully to prevent either of the parties from being alienated or, worse, allowed to seize control of the process and use it to force on the other spouse a unilaterally advantageous outcome.

There is also some danger that during this early phase one party will come to view the mediator as biased and will terminate the mediation. In most cases the parties bring a high level of tension, frustration, and anger into these early sessions; the mediator must constantly be monitoring their tolerance for this tension and finding ways to keep tensions at a level that will allow productive work to continue. This is not possible unless the mediator is firmly and comfortably in control of the process.

During this first hour of mediation Sue and Bob agreed to limit their initial negotiations, recognizing that it would be better not to finalize some issues until they had each had some experience of being a single parent and of living on a restricted budget. The current round of negotiations would focus on their separation: how they would arrange for both to spend time with the children, who would move out of the house, how they would meet their day-to-day expenses, and when they would develop and file a formal petition for a divorce. Long-term financial issues, including division of their assets, would be handled three months after they formally separated. From a mediator's point of view this was a desirable decision, for it is often very hard to help couples reach realistic agreements on how they will function after they are divorced when they have no real knowledge of what their post-separation circumstances will be. It is hard to project the impact of new housing arrangements, schedules, children's needs and reactions, and very real fiscal restraints.

The primary issues framed above were stated differently in that first hour of mediation. As in most mediations, the parties' initial comments were almost exclusively position statements. Bob's initial statement was, "I will not move out of the house; I love my kids and they need me." Sue's response to this was, "Of course you love the kids, and they love you, but they sure don't see much of you now. I can't stand it when you act so priggy. Of course you are going to leave, or my lawyer will have you thrown out." It was the mediator's job to help reframe these, and similar comments, into resolvable issues:

- If the Salkins were not to live together, alternate housing would need to be found, and paid for, for one of them.
- When they were no longer living together, different arrangements would have to be made to ensure that they both had time with the children.

Similarly a heated discussion about money led to several general principles that would govern their separate and mutual financial responsibilities during the mediation period.

- In order to preserve their current financial options they would need to find a way to ensure that neither party could unilaterally expend large sums of money, or incur large debts, until a formal fiscal separation had been agreed on.
- The interim and final arrangements would have to leave both of them, and their children, feeling that they could live with the arrangements and that their basic needs would be taken care of.
- They would need to devise a way of keeping their individual expenses separate, perhaps by establishing new individual accounts, and agree on how much they could spend each month.

The Salkins disagree about solutions, but at least they could agree on what the issues were. They also agreed that they would take the time to explore how best to resolve the questions both felt were important. By the end of this first hour, they had been able to consider briefly all the major areas they would need to address prior to drafting a formal agreement, and had agreed on what additional information they would need before the next meeting. A tentative schedule was set for subsequent mediation sessions, and they were asked to phone the mediator to discuss any individual concerns about trying to work out these issues in mediation. They were told that they would be asked, among other questions, whether physical or substance abuse was an issue in their family that would have to be addressed in mediation.

Each of the Salkins, like others before them, had expressed surprise that the other party was interested in trying to meet that person's needs. Sue had said that this was the first time she had heard Bob say he valued all she had done for the children, and that he was willing to work toward ending the marriage. Bob had responded that he had thought Sue was interested only in severing her relationship with him, and that she cared little for his relationship with the children. As with many other couples these positive statements initially were made quite tentatively and often were buried in several negative points. It took careful attention and work on the mediator's part to identify and isolate the positive statements, and then to get them repeated and heard by the other parent.

From the mediator's point of view, this first introductory session had gone well. There appeared to be no reason not to continue with the mediation. The Salkins had been quite angry with each other, but their hostility had been tinged with some hopeful signs. They had a history of being able to resolve disputes, or at least a history of acquiescing in the other's wishes. They did not relish their current conflict.

In the early stages of any mediation, much time is spent clarifying what is being said and reexamining issues in a way that will permit resolution later. It is the mediator's job to keep firmly in mind that this couple is negotiating an agreement that ultimately will have to pass judicial scrutiny, and that this agreement will have to address fully the needs of the whole family, adults and children. The mediator must be able to help the family draw on their past history and experience, while actively encouraging them to negotiate a forward-looking and realistic agreement. Although some aspects of a final agreement will be open to revision, changes in the agreement may well be harder to achieve than the couple believes. Many of the specifics, notably the division of property and other assets, will be essentially fixed once the divorce is final.

Each separating or divorcing family negotiates both in the light of its own needs and in the light of public policy, which is often expressed in statutory and case law as interpreted by the court that would hear any formal legal petition. When divorcing parents appear to expect or consider an outcome that is likely to violate current community standards or be antithetical to the children's needs, it is the mediator's obligation to encourage them to seek the advice and counsel of an outside expert or of their own advocate before the questionable proposal becomes an accepted base for their negotiations.

As the mediation proceeds, and as successive issues are examined to illuminate the parties' needs and interests, it will become apparent to the couple that they are, to quote Mnookin, "bargaining in the shadow of the law."[13] At any time, one of the parties might come to believe that he or she would do better before a judge, and so decide to end the mediation effort and go to court. The other party might, of course, under his or her lawyer's direction, come to agree that the spouse would indeed prevail in a trial and alter his or her position to allow the mediation effort to continue. Many couples do not particularly care how a judge might decide an issue, feeling that it is their right to resolve their affairs in a way that is sensible to them. However, the couple will come to realize that they are bargaining in the shadow not only of the law, but of their own family history, of the realities of their financial circumstances, and perhaps of their shared societal or religious values. All these external realities gradually impinge on their hopes and aspirations, circumscribing the shape of their final agreement.

One of the real strengths of mediation is that it does allow both parties to look forward. They can draw on the past for suggestions on avoiding future difficulties, without unduly focusing on the past to assess blame. This strength, however, can be a real weakness when both societal needs expressed in public policy and individual needs require the assignment of blame or accountability based on past behavior. For the Salkins' mediation to continue, Bob would have to put aside his anger at Sue for deciding to end the marriage. He would not be able to use her decision as an overt or covert bargaining chip in

---

[13]Mnookin & Kornhauser, *Bargaining in the Shadow of the Law: The Case of Divorce*, 88 YALE L. J. 950 (1979).

their negotiations. Sue could get her separation and divorce eventually without Bob's active help. Mediation is not a good option for a spouse seeking retribution for the other's past indifference or adultery. Unless both parties agree that some past actions require special consideration for the aggrieved spouse, blame has a small role in mediation.

Some behavior, such as alcoholism, might require the mediator to terminate his or her involvement in the negotiations —if, for instance, the alcoholic refused to accept responsibility for past behavior and to acknowledge the possible future damage should the drinking continue. It is not the fact itself that someone drinks to excess that dictates termination, but rather the drinker's inability to allow the drinking to be considered as one of many factors in the negotiations. Few parents would or should be willing to have their children in a car with a person who has been drinking. If the pattern is acknowledged, perhaps the children could see this parent at a time of day when she or he does not drink, with transportation back and forth provided by the other parent.

If in the Salkin case, there had been allegations that Sue was abusing one or more of the children, or that Bob was abusing Sue, and these allegations were denied, the mediation would have had to be terminated unless a mutually acceptable way could have been devised to confirm or dismiss the charges. Were they true, an expert would have had to be called in to assess the full implications of the abuse, and to help the couple devise not only a treatment plan but an agreement to ensure the safety of all the individuals involved. What constitutes abuse and whether someone is being abused are never appropriate subjects for mediation. Nor is mediation ever used to reach an agreement delineating circumstances under which abuse is an appropriate reaction.

In most disputes, the balance of power is not equal. And power in most families is balanced differently in different areas. The Salkins were no exception. Bob was at a disadvantage in two major respects: in his relative lack of parenting experience, and in not being emotionally ready for the separation. Sue, while understanding well the family's household finances, was not at all sure of her own employability and future earnings; she was going to have to rely on Bob financially for some time to come. But in this case, power could be realigned by the mediator's careful balancing of the timing and flow of information, and by separating the process of exploration from the process of decision-making. Sue was ready to have Bob spend more time with the children than he had been spending; he in turn welcomed Sue's willingness to offer him both guidance and a planned, phased-in, larger role for him in the children's lives. Bob had not realized that Sue not only knew that she would need to return to work but welcomed the chance to do so; and he appeared ready to reorganize their family finances.

In a very real sense, the Salkins had already arrived at a successful mediation outcome. They had agreed on the issues they needed to address and had set a time frame for their resolution while stabilizing interim arrangements. Subsequent benchmarks of success would include articulating why they disagreed, developing objective criteria for resolving their differences, and finally, resolving all the issues that needed to be addressed prior to formalizing their agreement.

In brief private conversations with each party, the mediator again reviewed their options and asked if there were issues that they had been reluctant to raise in the initial meeting for fear of jeopardizing the mediation. It transpired that there were no hidden issues; if there were, special help might have been required to ensure that these concerns were handled productively in any future negotiations.

In private the Salkins both had expressed relief that they were working cooperatively, as they feared of some of the unilateral options that their lawyers had raised: the closing down of charge cards or unilaterally moving joint savings and checking accounts into an escrow account. These and similar actions, while possibly legally prudent, may seriously discolor the couple's subsequent negotiations and often lead to an almost insurmountable erosion of trust. In this case, having been 'educated' by their lawyers, both parties were willing to devise a cooperative plan that met their own self-interest as well as their lawyer's concerns. They were bringing legal advice into the mediation and using it to establish the limits within which they would devise a cooperative, essentially fair solution; this model is one that the Salkins would return to frequently.

At the end of the second mediation session, the Salkins had reached an agreement that met both their own and their lawyers' concerns. Bob would move out within two weeks. He and Sue would continue to be jointly responsible for making all major decisions regarding the children (Bob would be more active in future), they would both spend prescheduled times with the children, and call upon each other if they needed a temporary respite. Their finances were redistributed slightly to allow Bob to rent an apartment and Sue to establish her own account and a line of credit, but each had agreed to make no major expenditures, nor incur any large debts, without the other's prior approval. The house and the balance of their savings were to be off limits to both of them pending the next round of negotiations, which were scheduled to begin in three months. The agreement was also worded to ensure that neither of them gained nor lost any real advantage in terms of their final divorce by having cooperated to achieve this mutually agreed-on separation.

The dynamics and substance of this mediation can perhaps be best understood in terms of Fisher and Ury's *Getting to Yes*[14] (see TABLE 1). Both Bob and Sue were helped to move from their initial hard positional statements, regarding both the children and the house, to statements that reflected their true needs and interests. This was achieved by helping them clarify their assumptions and hidden perceptions. The final elements of the agreement, based largely on the objective criteria that flowed from their joint and separate needs, were then achieved with relative ease. The Salkins might have been able to arrive at this point on their own if they had not been so emotionally embroiled in the problem. Had their lawyers achieved this result for them, they might not have had quite the same investment in upholding the agreement, and they would not have been in the relatively solid shape that they were in when they went into the next round of negotiations.

---

[14] R. Fisher & W. Ury, GETTING TO YES (1981).

TABLE 1.

Principled Family Negotiations*

	Husband	Wife
Position	a. I want joint custody. b. I am staying in the house.	I want sole custody. He has to leave the house.
Assumption	a. If I don't have joint legal custody, I won't have any input, or say, in my kids' lives and upbringing. b. If I leave, I will lose my home and my children for ever.	If I don't have sole legal custody, he will continue to try to run my life for me, controlling me. If he leaves, life will be much less stressful for all of us.
Perception	a. She does not want me to play an active role in raising the children. b. She is using the stress issues as a lever to get me out. She knows that I care about the children's well-being.	He does not want me to be an independent person. He is staying just to protect his financial interests. He doesn't really care about me or the children.
Interest	a. To make it possible for us to continue our mutual responsibility for all areas of our children's lives. b. To retain my financial interests in the house.	To lead a life that is separate from his control but not to exclude him from the children's lives. To separate now, and to work out the financial details later.

*With acknowledgements to Roger Fisher and William Ury

TABLE 1. *(continued)*

	Husband	*Wife*
<u>*Objective Criteria*</u>	a. Meaningful relationship with children and input into decision-making.	Meaningful separation of parent/spouse roles.
	b. No loss of legal standing by moving out.	Firm date for husband to move out of the house.

Before continuing with the Salkins' saga, let us examine some of the theoretical underpinnings of mediation. As previously noted, mediation gains much of its strength through the mediator's careful management of the conflict between the disputing parties. Morton Deutsch[15] has described two broad types of conflict resolution: a cooperative (constructive) model, and a competitive (destructive) model. The latter is characterized by poor communications, frequently designed to mislead or intimidate the other party; and by one or both parties pushing for a single option, often in an attempt to gain or retain a power imbalance. Both tactics which generate additional conflict over who has the power to impose her or his solution. Successive rounds of these destructive behaviors produce a climate of mistrust and anger that goads each party to minimize any possibility of acknowledging similarities. Differences are exaggerated and can soon lead to actions that wildly exceed personal and community norms. It is not unusual during a divorce, for instance, for people to start to feel that they have a right, if not an obligation, to open another person's mail without consent, eavesdrop on phone conversations, and even turn their children into spies.

Mediation approaches the family's conflict with a cooperative, constructive resolution method. The parties replace their current lack of trust in each other with trust in the mediator's ability to help them stick to a process that will result in a fair

---

[15]M. Deutsch, THE RESOLUTION OF CONFLICT (1973).

outcome. To achieve this, they have to grant to the mediator the initial right to manage their communications within the mediation sessions, give up the hope for unilateral, single-resolution options, and begin to accept that as members of a family, albeit a divorced one, they have many more similarities than differences. The mediator has to find a way to recreate a level of mutual trust sufficiently high to make it possible for the parties to move forward and cooperatively restructure their obligations. The mediator must then gradually return control of the process to the parties to fashion an agreement that makes sense for them.

One significant potential benefit of mediation is that the family need not make the trade-offs that are often a part of adversarial negotiations. College is not offset by current primary school education costs or cost-of-living escalation clauses, orthodonture is not offset by uninsured medical costs. All of the factors are considered sequentially, understood, and then dealt with as part of a final package. Indeed, one of the real advantages of the mediator's neutral role is that he or she can develop and present a series of packaged solutions, options based on a thorough understanding of the family's individual needs and interests and shaped by a realistic assessment of what each parent can accept. Each can, and usually does, offer modifications that would better meet his or her needs, thus leading to further mutual understanding of their position. Often a package is acceptable even though it would have been rejected had it been proposed earlier in the process or by one of the parties.

The mediator has the opportunity to put forward imaginative resolutions based on her or his extensive knowledge of the subject and particular knowledge of the family. Often these hypothetical options will serve to move a couple away from imminent deadlock by expanding their horizons. Equity in a house that neither parent could afford to buy from the other might be decreased by placing part of the equity in an escrow fund for the children's college expenses. A new health insurance policy might be found, at a slight increase in premium, to cover all dental care including orthodonture with no charges above the premium.

Other third-party dispute resolution options can achieve a similar final agreement, but these other methods cannot leave the parties with the same sense of ownership and commitment. An attorney required to represent a single party's best interests would have to work extremely hard, with another very cooperative lawyer, to maintain the openness that the constructive model requires. A knowledgable therapist might well help a divorcing couple reach a somewhat similar agreement, but it is likely that a therapist's training would lead to a focus on primarily psychotherapeutic concerns rather than pragmatic realities. For discussion of the range of options available to a divorcing couple, see Goldberg, Green, and Sander,[16] and Kressel's new book, *The Processes of Divorce*[17].

The Salkins, like many other couples, easily could have slipped into escalating rounds of mistrust and anger. Bob might have gone ahead with his lawyer's suggestion that he place all the Salkins' joint assets out of Sue's reach in an escrow account. Then Sue undoubtedly would have come up with an equally unilateral reaction, perhaps by magnifying Bob's relative inaction as a parent and attempting to deny him a continuing and meaningful role in raising their children. The Salkins were a typically angry and frustrated couple: unsure of their options, each unsure about the other's reactions and responses to requests, and often unsure about what exactly they wanted.

Mediation provided the Salkins with a safe environment for exploring all their questions and beginning to understand what they needed and wanted in their restructured lives. Their communications, while controlled by the mediator, were always direct and nearly always made in the presence of the other party; there was little chance of random miscommunications sabotaging the negotiations. Throughout the process, their lawyers and other advisers had the opportunity to help them explore their individual and joint needs, and to coach them in the end stages as the final language of their interim agreement became set. They would find it easier to negotiate the

---

[16] S. B. Goldberg, E. D. Green & F. E. A. Sander, DISPUTE RESOLUTION (1985).

[17] K. Kressel, THE PROCESSES OF DIVORCE (1985).

remaining issues now that they had become familiar with the dispute resolution process.

The Salkins' second round of mediator-assisted negotiations began on schedule three months later and lasted for an additional five-hour spread over three sessions. They arrived well-prepared with current estimates of the market value of their house, present values of their pensions, and a realistic understanding of their financial needs. In the interim, Sue had obtained assurances about a future teaching position and knew what her income would be over the next few years and what hours she would not be available to supervise the children. They were both familiar now with the pattern of being cooperative single parents of two active children. They had both come to realize that in many ways their schedules would have to take second place to their children's schedules if they were to enjoy a harmonious relationship with their children. Bob, for instance, suggested that he take over primary responsibility for scheduling and taking the children to the dentist and orthodontist: appointments that by and large would have to take place while Sue was teaching. They were both concerned about providing adequate supervision for Gail when she was ill and had to stay out of school, and getting Tom to all the after-school activities he wanted to enjoy with his friends. By now these were problems to solve, not manifestations of the worth or lack of worth of the other parent.

As in the initial mediation when they devised their interim agreement, the Salkins got helped in drawing up a complete list of areas they would need to address. Each of these areas was fully discussed and explored before attempting to resolve any one of them. The work went faster than before because the Salkins were increasingly skilled at framing their concerns in ways that permitted several possible resolutions. They had learned to separate their interests from their desired outcome and to check their assumptions about the other's position before acting on any unverified assumption.

Following the first session, there was a brief delay while each obtained additional facts and figures. Between the penultimate and final session there was also a three-week interruption that the Salkins used to go over their proposed agreement with their lawyers and with their tax accountant to ensure that the agreement met the objective criteria agreed on. This final agreement, known as a "memorandum of understanding," was to be incorporated into the formal divorce petition and the subsequent legal proceedings by Sue's lawyer, subject, of course, to the scrutiny and approval of Bob's lawyer.

The role of an attorney advising clients who are choosing to negotiate for themselves within the framework of mediation is not an easy one. The lawyer will be asked to make a realistic assessment of the potential outcome if the dispute were to be litigated, and the lawyer's answer will undoubtedly affect the course of the negotiations. These predictions are difficult to make particularly in the area of family law, but they will be necessary, eventually, and they are easier to make once the family has fully defined their circumstances, needs, and financial resources. The attorney's role becomes more that of a teacher and counselor than of an advocate. It is often hard to balance whether or not a client should attempt to obtain a slightly higher financial share of a house or pension at the cost of a severely strained interparent or interchild relationship. It is hard to assess the benefits of possibly better compliance against current short-term gains. It is hard for a professional who has spent a lifetime advising and acting as advocate to step back and let the client choose an outcome that the professional believes is not truly in the client's best interests.

Despite all these difficulties, there is encouragement in Jessica Pearson's[18] research. Her studies found that in general, the children of families that went through mediation saw their noncustodial parent more often than did the children of families that had not negotiated for themselves. She found, too, that this noncustodial parent paid slightly higher monthly amounts of child support. While both the amount of time and the amount of support decreased over the subsequent year, they changed less than in the nonmediation group. Mediation is still a relatively new field, and it will take years to learn whether these positive results hold up for long periods. We do

---

[18] J. Pearson, The Denver Custody Mediation Project: Final Report (Center for Policy Research, Denver, Colorado).

know that approximately 20 percent of the families who have followed a more traditional, court-focused route to reach an agreement return to court to either modify or enforce the terms of an existing agreement[19].

Relitigation rates probably represent only the tip of an iceberg of discontent. Both academic and popular writings are replete with descriptions of the numerous difficulties many families experience, first in their attempts to obtain a just divorce settlement and then in living within the constraints of these arrangements. Mediation can help some families forge an agreement that they believe is fair, reasonable, and workable, and therefore has a better chance of working to the long-time satisfaction of the whole family.

---

[19]Phear, Clark, Hauser, Whitney & Beck, *An Empirical Study of Custody Agreements: Joint Versus Sole Legal Custody*, 11 J. PSYCHIATRY & LAW 419.

CHAPTER NINE
Negotiating Settlements of Property, Alimony and Child Support

—————— H. Joseph Gitlin ——————

This chapter analyzes the stages of settling the issues of property, alimony, and child support, examining these issues from the perspective of both husband and wife and applying a hypothetical set of facts to the justification of a settlement. Specific means of settling difficult problems are suggested. Using this chapter as a roadmap can lead to a successful, fair settlement of these three often-recurring issues.

A successful negotiation of these matters involves maximum negotiating leverage as well as creativity in developing attractive alternatives when an apparent impasse is reached.

While it is not the purpose of this chapter to discuss specific negotiating techniques to gain leverage for your side, keep in mind that virtually everything the lawyer and client do during the divorce process will have an impact on their leverage. For example, if you perceive that either for want of evidence or want of skill, the other side is not in a good position to try the case, this boosts your negotiating leverage. The primary way to gain leverage is to demonstrate to the other side the strengths and justifiability of your negotiating positions and your ability to take the case to trial if necessary.

The lawyer's insensitivity to the other side's positions may adversely affect the negotiating process. The client's insensitivity to the emotions of the other spouse—for instance, being open about an extramarital relationship—may also negatively affect settlement.

As a lawyer handling a divorce case, you are working on a dual track. On one track is trial preparation; on the other track is the negotiating process. In trial preparation you gather the data and law needed to try the case, while simultanteously the other side is being convinced of the litigation strength of your case.

The first step, one that should continue throughout the negotiating process, is to convince the client to seek a fair agreement. Each position the lawyer and client take must be rational and capable of justification. The negotiating process begins with thus, the lawyer's first interview with the client.

THE FIVE STAGES OF A DIVORCE CASE

You should not start the actual settlement negotiations before you have sufficient data. The steps to bringing a case to a conclusion are:

- Fact gathering (both from your client and through discovery).
- Cataloging and categorizing the facts.
- Evaluation of the financial data.
- Negotiations.
- The settlement agreement itself or trial.

In all but those cases in which there are no significant assets, it will take at least several months for the lawyer to acquire sufficient information to start the negotiations.

THE TYPICAL FACTS: A HYPOTHETICAL

For the purpose of this chapter we will consider a typical divorce case: There are two children of school age; both parties are employed, with the husband earning a larger income than the wife; and the major assets are the marital residence and the husband's pension plan.

We will consider alternative family structures in which the husband's employment income is from a closely held corporation or from a profession. Additional typical assets, such as Individual Retirement Accounts and tax shelters, will also be considered.

FAIRNESS AND CONSISTENCY: THE BENCHMARKS OF GOOD SETTLEMENTS

Fairness as a benchmark of marital settlement agreements is not just an ideological platitude. It is practical. When children are involved, as they are in the majority of divorces, the parties will continue to have a relationship with each other. It is rare that the entry of the divorce judgment effects a termination of the parties' need to have future communications. In most cases the parties to a divorce must communicate and cooperate, and this cannot be done effectively if one party feels grossly disadvantaged by the settlement agreement.

Developing a reputation for fairness and an ability and willingness to settle a divorce case also helps a lawyer's career. The reputation for fairness that lawyers develop precedes them from case to case.

With most divorce settlements negotiated by lawyers rather than imposed by a judge, lawyers engaging in divorce work should work out a consistent approach to settlement and apply this method to most of their cases. Nevertheless, they must be flexible enough to try an unusual approach in an unusual case.

An example of a consistent and fair approach to marital settlements can be posed in the area of life insurance to secure child support and alimony payments in the event of the obligor's premature death. These provisions are generally not a significant part of a marital settlement agreement unless the obligor dies. The ideal amount of life insurance, of course, is the amount that will satisfy the projected support obligation in the event of premature death; but in many divorce cases the ideal is not affordable. Sometimes no more life insurance than is currently in force is affordable. Settlement agreements often require the support obligor to keep all of his life insurance coverage for the benefit of the children or ex-wife. My consistent approach, although somewhat arbitrary, is that unless the ideal can be reached, the support obligor should retain control of 25 percent of his life insurance coverage to provide for his last illness and burial and to allow some coverage for a future family of his own.

STEP ONE: DETERMINE PERCENTAGE DISTRIBUTION OF PROPERTY

The first consideration in forming a division of property is to estimate the percentage of marital property to be awarded to each party. Most jurisdictions, either by statute or case law, have a form of equitable distribution of property, that is, a fair division of the marital estate. In most such jurisdictions an equitable distribution is required, rather than a 50/50 division.

The model for equitable property distribution statutes is the Uniform Marriage and Divorce Act. The statutory scheme under the uniform act is first to distribute marital property and thereafter to make determinations of alimony and child support. The act provides that an award of alimony can be made only to a party who "lacks sufficient property to provide for his reasonable needs." Even though equitable distribution generally does not require a 50/50 division of marital property, for the sake of consistency in negotiating a divorce settlement a 50/50 division is the logical starting point, and then one can consider unusual factors suggesting some other division. A lawyer with a consistent reputation for a 50/50 division of marital property in the usual case will find it easier (in the unusual case) to negotiate a division other than 50/50.

Statutory Justification for Division of Property

The best way to negotiate a settlement dividing marital property along lines other than 50/50 is to justify your position on the basis of the law. What many lawyers overlook is the straightforward statutory law on distribution of property. For example, the Uniform Marriage and Divorce Act mentions that such factors as the age and health of a party may affect the apportionment of marital property. Thus the starting points for a justification of a disproportionate property division are the relevant statutory factors and interpretive case law.

Tax Consequences of Property Distribution

A major consideration in setting levels of alimony and child support is the tax consequence to each party. Under the recently amended Internal Revenue Code, the distribution of property pursuant to a divorce judgment is not a taxable event, that is, it has no immediate income tax consequences.

In representing an alimony and support recipient, it might be fair and practical to give that recipient a smaller amount of marital property in consideration for larger support and alimony payments that are tax deductible to the obligor. In effect, the support and alimony obligor would be paying for the spouse's share of marital property in tax-deductible dollars. But here it should be considered that the recipient will have to pay income tax on the amounts received; therefore, additional support and alimony should be provided for to cover the additional taxes.[1]

---

[1] Under the recently amended Internal Revenue Code, unallocated alimony and child support, which was formerly deductible, is now on its face not deductible. However, through creative drafting and cooperation between the parties, substantial income tax advantage can still be gained through the vehicle of paying deductible alimony.

Property in Lieu of Support and Alimony

When there is no assurance that future support obligations will be consistently met, for example, when the obligor has an inconsistent income pattern, it may be desirable for the support recipient to take a larger block of the property and smaller support payments. In a sense, what the support/alimony recipient is seeking is prepayment of all, or a part, of the future support/alimony obligation. A discount factor therefore should be built into the formula, because a dollar in hand is worth more than an anticipation of payments.

It should be noted that the property distribution will have an impact on the amount of alimony and child support. For example, the Uniform Marriage and Divorce Act states that in determining the length of alimony payments the court should consider "the financial resources of the party seeking maintenance (alimony) including marital property apportioned to him." Thus, for example, a dependent spouse who is entitled to $20,000 a year for her support receives as part of the distribution of marital property an asset capable of generating income of $8,000 per year. The alimony award should be reduced by $8,000, less the income tax to be paid on the $8,000.

We have now determined that in the usual case, marital property should be distributed on a 50/50 basis unless for practical reasons, and in accordance with the law, an unequal distribution should be made. In the negotiating process, the first step is to work out the theoretical percentage allocation of marital property between the parties. The next step, therefore, will be the more practical one of plugging in which assets go to whom.

WHO GETS WHAT AND WHY

In our hypothetical, the major assets are the marital residence and the husband's pension plan.

Divorcing parties, especially in smaller cases, tend to focus first on the division of household goods; the disposition of these goods is easier for them to conceptualize. The client should be advised that while the replacement value of household goods may be significant, their actual value is what they will bring at a garage sale and that consequently, the division of household goods may be left to last. The initial focus should be on the major assets.

The first considerations in determining who gets what are the relative needs of the parties and their children. Some questions must be asked.

Income-Producing Assets

Is it desirable for the support/alimony recipient to have income-producing assets? Is it desirable for this recipient to have retirement income, i.e., a part of the other spouse's pension plan? In the case of an elderly spouse with minimal employment skills, these factors must be considered.

The Pension Plan

If the values of the pension plan and the equity in the marital residence are nearly equal, is it desirable to trade one for the other?

Possession of the Residence

Is it desirable for the custodian of the children to remain in the marital residence at least for a time after the divorce? This decision has to be based on psychological and financial factors. For example, it may be psychologically desirable for the children of a divorcing couple to remain in the same marital home and school system to ease their adjustment to the divorce. It may also be practical if the payments on the marital residence are lower than rental or mortgage payments on another residence would be.

Dividing Sale Proceeds of the Residence—
Delayed Sale

If the sale of the marital residence and disposition of the proceeds are to be delayed for some time after the judgment, the eventual distribution of the proceeds from this asset involves some unique problems. It will be assumed in this example that the wife will have custody of the children and will be allowed to remain in the marital residence for five years. The real estate will then be sold and the proceeds divided between the parties, who have already agreed that each owns half the present equity in the real estate.

The husband's initial approach is simple but also simplistic. He wants the wife to make the mortgage payments, and when the real estate is sold he is to be paid half the equity. If he has a half interest, he says, he should have half the proceeds, but she should make the mortgage payments during the five years because she will be living there. He takes the position that this is fair because his money is being tied up for five years.

The wife's position is that she would be spending her money on the mortgage, and if the husband wants to share equally in the proceeds of the sale he should make half the mortgage payments.

Neither party's position is justifiable. A fair settlement of the disposition of the family residence should consider the following points:

- The husband is entitled to compensation because until the residence is sold, he will not have the use of an asset of which he is an equal owner.
- The wife should pay for the use of the value of the husband's half interest in the real estate.
- Since the marital residence is an asset that probably will fluctuate in value, the parties should share equally in the fluctuation.

The following formula will address these points:

FINANCIAL SETTLEMENTS

The real estate is valuated by an appraiser selected by the parties or by their attorneys. The parties agree that the fair market value of the real estate will be as determined by the appraisal. The mortgage balance is then deducted from the fair market value to determine the equity of the parties in the real estate. Each of the parties owns one-half of the equity at its present value. Thus the husband's present equity in the real estate is a fixed dollar amount. Upon the eventual sale, the value of the husband's interest in the real estate is determined as a ratio of the appraised value to the actual sale price.

To illustrate: The real estate is appraised at $160,000. The mortgage balance at the time of the judgment dissolving the marriage is $100,000; the value of the parties' equity is $60,000. If the husband's interest is 50 percent, then his present interest would be $30,000. The real estate eventually sells for $192,000, a 20 percent increase in the value of the home. The husband's interest of $30,000 would be increased by 20 percent, or $6,000, and he would therefore be paid $36,000 from the proceeds of the sale, less his equal share of the expenses of the sale. The wife would receive the balance of the proceeds of the sale.

An alternative means of compensating the husband for delaying receipt of his interest in the family residence is for the wife simply to pay him interest on his share of the equity. This, however, can raise income tax problems if the interest is to be paid out of the proceeds of the sale, since it may give the husband a substantial amount of ordinary income in one year, inordinately raising his income tax. The preferred way, from the husband's perspective, would be for the wife to pay the husband interest on an annual basis.

"Immediate" Sale of Residence

Even if the real estate is to be sold "immediately," it is not likely that the sale will actually be immediate. Even in a good market, selling a residence will usually take several months. This delay raises problems to be resolved in the negotiating process:

- At what price shall the residence be listed?
- What happens if the residence is not sold at the listed price within a reasonable time?
- Who will occupy the residence until sale?
- What if the party in occupancy is not motivated to sell?
- Who will make the mortgage payment until the property is sold?
- Who will pay for the necessary repairs and maintenance of the residence until it is sold?

The negotiating solutions to the problems are:

- If the parties cannot agree to a listing price, it should be determined by an appraiser selected either by the parties or their lawyers.
- The listing price should be inflated somewhat (perhaps 10 percent) over the appraised value to leave room for negotiations. It can be provided that if the property does not sell within a certain amount of time, the price will be lowered. A well-negotiated and well-drafted settlement would provide for the price to be lowered by a certain amount, or certain percentage, periodically at the insistence of either party. Below a certain point both parties would have to agree to a further reduction, and any offer that meets or exceeds the agreed-upon sale price (as adjusted from time to time) would have to be accepted at the insistence of either party.
- Under some marital settlement formulas, it may be financially advantageous to the spouse who remains in the marital residence to continue residing there, and it should then be anticipated that this spouse may not be fully cooperative in selling the house. A well-drafted agreement, therefore, will have a provision requiring the remaining spouse to cooperate with brokers in the sale of the residence and keeping the residence repaired and attractive.

FINANCIAL SETTLEMENTS

If under the settlement formula, the nonresident spouse is contributing to the mortgage or paying all of it, a formula could be worked out for reductions in that spouse's contribution towards the mortgage if the real estate does not sell in a certain amount of time, thus giving the remaining spouse an incentive to cooperate in the sale of the residence.

- Mortgage payments until the residence is sold cause the most significant problem.

Assume that each of the parties has an employment income but that neither party alone can afford to pay the mortgage, especially considering the nonoccupant spouse's obligation to pay for his or her own living quarters. Assume further that the wife has agreed to stay in the marital residence until it is sold. The husband's position is that if she is residing there, she should pay the mortgage. The wife's position is that she cannot afford to pay the mortgage, and that if she paid the entire mortgage the husband would be taking advantage of the principal mortgage reduction without having contributed to it. The wife also claims that she had planned to rent a residence and that the rental would be lower than the mortgage payments. The husband responds that the wife would have to pay rent wherever she goes, and therefore she should pay the mortgage.

If the mortgage payments are $1,000 per month, while a place that the wife could rent would cost her $500 per month, a fair settlement would try to achieve the following:

- The wife would contribute to the mortgage an amount equal to what she would have to pay for rent if she moved.

- Each of the parties should contribute to the balance of the mortgage payments because they will be sharing equally in the proceeds of the sale.

- Attention must also be given to the cost of necessary repairs and maintenance of the family residence until it is sold. Since both parties will be sharing equally in the proceeds of the sale, such expenses should be shared equally. If the proceeds were not to be equally shared, the expenses should be paid in ratio to the division of the proceeds of the sale.

The Pension Plan Is Marital Property

The disposition of a pension plan—or any other type of deferred income plan, such as profit-sharing or retirement plan—raises complex valuation and decisional problems.

When representing the owner of a pension plan, the lawyer's first task is to convince the client that indeed the pension plan is part of the marital estate. The problem with the client is somewhat akin to the problems lawyers had in the 1960s, when state statutes imposed stiff jail sentences for possession of minimal amounts of marijuana. When the lawyer advised the client of the penalties for possession of several grams of marijuana, the usual response of the client was, "Hey man, like you gotta be kidding!" Clients, when told their pension plan is marital property, have similar responses. This is especially true with senior, upper-income, corporate employees who have pension plans with substantial value.

To the extent it was earned during the marriage, the plan is indeed a part of the marital estate.

The Value of the Pension Plan

If the plan is a defined contribution plan following the requirements of federal law, the plan owner will have received within the past twelve months a printout of the amounts of money contributed to the plan. The client may therefore assume that the value of the plan is the amount of money currently in the plan. That, however, is not the present cash value of the plan.

"You've gotta be kidding!" the client will say once again. When lawyers started dealing with pension plans as marital property, they treated them like any other asset: They were quick to hire an expert, an actuary, to give them the present cash value of a pension plan (which is a promise to pay money upon retirement). When lawyers found through the actuary that the present cash value of a pension plan was substantially more than the actual money deposited into the plan, the pension-owning client reacted with even more consternation.

If the settlement is based on what has been contributed to the plan, the pension-owning client is well-served. If, however, the non-pension-owning spouse wishes a settlement based on the present cash value of the pension plan, an actuarial opinion is required.

The "If and When" Disposition of a Pension Plan

As, however, courts of review began considering actuarial opinions on the value of pension plans, they became aware that such opinions were, in part, guesswork based on statistics. For example, one of the projections an actuary makes in determining present cash value of a pension plan is the percentage rate of profit the capital investment in the pension plan will earn in the future. One percentage point of difference in this projection can make many thousands of dollars' difference in the present cash value of the plan. Courts of review have therefore recently leaned to an "if and when" standard for the disposition of pension plans: The non-pension-owning spouse is awarded benefits under the pension plan if the pension-owning spouse gets benefits from the plan, and on the same basis as the pension-owning spouse. The appellate courts have urged this approach in particular when the plan is not vested and there is a possibility that the pension-owning spouse may never, because of death or termination of current employment, gain any benefits from the pension plan.

One of the problems of the "if and when" approach to pension plans was that as a matter of federal law, pension plans are not assignable, and therefore the non-pension-owning spouse had to rely on the other spouse to make payments out of the plan in accordance with the court's order. This problem was solved by new federal law authorizing QDROs (Qualified

Domestic Relations Orders), which in effect make the pension plan administrator a party to the order and require that administrator to make payments directly to the non-pension-owning spouse.

The representative of the non-pension owning spouse may be tempted to negotiate for the present cash value of the pension plan because it gives the spouse up-front money. If, however, this spouse does not own any retirement plan and, moreover, because of age, health, or lack of future employment is unlikely to acquire an adequate pension plan, serious consideration should be given to providing the client an interest in the other spouse's pension plan.

If there is an actuarial evaluation of the pension plan, the lawyer negotiating for the pension-owning spouse should try to bring down the actuarial evaluation. Ways to attack the actuarial value are suggested in an article by James T. Friedman.[2]

Trading Off the Pension Plan

Assuming that the major assets are a pension plan and the marital residence, settlement of the property issues involves setting off the values of these assets against each other.

If both parties have pension plans and the plans are nearly equal in value, the settlement is easy. Each party keeps his and her own pension plan with adjustments for any substantial differences. If only one of the parties has a pension plan, the trade-off is the house against the pension plan, with adjustments for the difference in values.

Difficulties in Evaluating an Interest in Closely Held Corporation or Professional Practice

Disposition of a spouse's interest in a closely held corporation or a profession is among the more complex tasks in a

---

[2] *Questions to Trap the Expert,* FAM. ADVOC., Fall, 1985, at 24.

divorce settlement. The evaluation of such assets requires technical expertise and is usually performed by accountants.

Determining the tangible assets of a closely held corporation or professional practice is a relatively easy task. What is complex is giving a value to the stock of a closely held corporation because the stock is not sold in the marketplace. This also applies to determining the good will value of a professional practice. The evaluation by an expert of a closely held corporation or professional practice (much the same as evaluation of a pension plan by an actuary) seems to be scientific up to a certain point. The expert starts with actual figures taken from the books of the business or professional practice, but later a multiplier is introduced and justified on the basis of custom and usage, IRS formulas, etc. The multiplier factor is the soft side of the formula and should be carefully examined in the negotiating process. It can make hundreds of thousands of dollars' difference.

Keep in mind that the value of an assignment of the shares of stock in a closely held corporation is dubious. The spouse receiving stock will undoubtedly be a minority shareholder, and benefits from the ownership of this stock will be controlled by the majority. The spouse outside the corporation is better served by receiving the value of the shares of stock, rather than the stock.

Are Elements of a Professional Practice Income or Property?

In dealing with a professional practice, the lawyer for the nonprofessional spouse should examine whether the client will be better served by taking the position that certain elements of the practice are marital property, the value of which can be divided now between the parties, or by treating such assets as income to be a basis for child support and alimony. Depending on the jurisdiction's law, such elements of a practice as the degree and the license to practice may or may not be treated as property. In the case of other professionals, such as artists and authors, royalties may be considered as property. For example, in the divorce case of Charles M. Schulz, the author of the cartoon strip "Peanuts," the Tax Court held that the royalties he received from his strip were property.

Obviously, when there will be no child support or alimony, the non-property-owning spouse is best served by attempting to negotiate a settlement in which as many assets as possible are treated as property and thus divisible between the parties.

Individual Retirement Accounts

If an employed spouse and an unemployed spouse both have IRAs, typically the employed spouse's IRA will be larger than the other's. The IRS has ruled that IRAs may be rolled over from one spouse to another without losing tax deductibility. The division of IRAs between the spouses should be an easy matter.

Distribution of Tax Shelters

The distribution of tax shelters within a settlement requires more than superficial attention. Obviously a tax shelter is worth more to the spouse with the higher income, and therefore the tax shelter should ordinarily go to that spouse. The tax shelter is usually worth more than its face value, or purchase price, because its value depends on the tax savings it brings to the owner.

The spouse with lower income should try to maximize the value of the plan by demonstrating significant tax savings that result from ownership of the shelter. The spouse with higher income should argue the reverse. This spouse may emphasize the smaller tax advantage to the lower-income spouse and may also emphasize that the shelter could even turn out to be a financial liability—for example, in tax shelter limited partnerships, the partnership may impose an assessment on the partners.

Thus it may be simplistic to approach tax shelters like any other asset of fixed value to be divided equally between the parties.

ALIMONY

There are two steps in the consideration of alimony: is the spouse entitled to alimony, and if so, how much and for how long?

Under the Uniform Marriage and Divorce Act, a spouse is entitled to alimony if she "lacks sufficient property to provide for her reasonable needs and is unable to support herself through appropriate employment [or] is the custodian of a child whose condition or circumstances make it appropriate that the custodian not be required to seek employment outside of the home." These and other statutory and case law factors should be weighed.

Income-Producing Property

The first question is whether the alimony-seeking spouse, as a result of the anticipated settlement, will have sufficient potentially income-producing assets to support herself. If, for example, the wife requires a $50,000 gross income per year to support herself, and the anticipated settlement will give her $500,000 in assets that can be invested at 10 percent, she will need no alimony.

The second possibility is that the wife will have income-producing assets but that the income the property can produce falls short of meeting her needs. She needs alimony to meet the shortfall.

In a third scenario, the wife will receive no income-producing assets. This wife's needs must be met by alimony alone.

The husband may want to formulate a settlement giving the wife the maximum in potentially income-producing assets, in order to eliminate or minimize his obligation for alimony (unless it is advantageous for income tax reasons to pay alimony rather than give property). It should be determined whether, upon a divorce, keeping the marital residence is possible within the wife's budget. Assume, for example, that as a result of trade-offs, the wife is to have as her own a marital residence with $150,000 in equity. The husband's lawyer should urge that she sell the residence if for $75,000 she can purchase a residence adequate for her needs, thus giving her $75,000 to produce income. This would reduce the husband's obligation for alimony.

Wife's Employment Income

Another factor to consider for entitlement to alimony is a wife's ability to support herself through appropriate employment. Here it would be urged in negotiations that she should not be required to work at a demeaning job at the minimum wage.

Effect of Being Custodian of Children

The third factor to consider in determining whether a spouse should receive alimony is whether she is the custodian of children and should not be required to seek employment outside of the home. The wife would press this factor when, because of the children, she has not been employed, and the husband has the means to support her during the period when it is appropriate for her to devote her attention to the children. The husband, on the other hand, would argue that the wife's unemployment is an unaffordable luxury.

Tax Consequences of Alimony

If by virtue of the statutory and case law, it appears that the wife is entitled to alimony, the next step in the negotiating process is to consider the statutory and case law factors regarding the amount of alimony and the length of time for which it should be paid.

The decisional law in many jurisdictions is that the court should consider the income tax consequences to the parties of an award of alimony. The tax consequences are probably the single most influential factor in negotiating the amount and the period of alimony payments.

FINANCIAL SETTLEMENTS

Even when a wife is not entitled to alimony, it may be wise to pay a property distribution obligation in that form because alimony is tax-deductible to the payor, while a distribution of property within divorce proceedings is not a taxable event.

The alimony recipient should emphasize that the payor is receiving a tax deduction for the alimony payments and that the recipient has to pay taxes on the alimony.

The manner of presenting the tax savings to the alimony payor is significant. For example, the taxpayer with taxable income of approximately $85,000 is in a bracket where the overall federal income tax is approximately 35 percent. However, on the top $17,000 or so of income, the taxes are approximately 48 percent. Thus, the negotiator for the alimony recipient should emphasize that the alimony payor is saving almost 50 cents on the dollar. That negotiator should also stress that the gross amount of alimony should not only cover the client's needs but should include an additional amount to cover income taxes on the alimony itself.

The Prospective Budgets of Each Party

The basic tool for both husband and wife in determining what the amount of alimony should be is for each to prepare a prospective budget showing his or her needs after the divorce. It is important to advise the client that these needs should be measured in accordance with the lifestyle of the parties during the marriage.

In negotiating the amount of alimony, and in negotiating the amount of child support as well, care should be taken that the client's budget is realistic and is based on the lifestyle of the parties. The budget should neither be minimal, reflecting the frugalities that had to be exercised recently, nor should it be exaggerated. An exaggerated budget can come back to haunt you. If the husband claims he is spending $600 per month on food for himself, then the wife, who has custody of two teenage children, might very well argue that she is entitled to $1,800 per month for food expenditures.

If some amount of time has gone by during the negotiating

process in which the wife has been living on a lesser amount than she is seeking in the final settlement, the focus for the potential alimony payor should be on the wife's ability to manage adequately with the amounts she has been receiving. The alimony recipient, however, should urge that she has attempted to work within the amounts she was given, but that these amounts do not allow the lifestyle that the parties maintained during the marriage.

The Concept of Rehabilitative Alimony

The Uniform Marriage and Divorce Act and most state divorce acts do not spell out the concept of "rehabilitative alimony," but that concept is recognized by case law in many jurisdictions. It grows out of statutory factors used to determine (1) whether there should be an award of alimony (whether the spouse is "unable to support herself through appropriate employment") and (2) the amount and period of alimony payments ("the time necessary to acquire sufficient education or training to enable the party seeking alimony to find appropriate employment").

The interpretive case law holds that the alimony recipient, if she is able to do so, has an obligation to seek appropriate employment to meet her full income-earning potential. If and when she reaches that potential, she is no longer entitled to alimony, but to the extent that her full income potential leaves her with a lower standard of living than she experienced during the marriage, the husband will be required to continue paying alimony.

If the wife was formerly unemployed, the focus for her should be on what "appropriate employment" is. If appropriate employment requires that she receive training or education, the amount of alimony should reflect not only the support of the wife but also her educational or training expenses.

For the husband, the focus should be on the rehabilitative nature of alimony. He would urge that his obligation should be for a fixed and short period of time, rather than in perpetuity. On the other hand, the wife should urge, as case law has held, that to provide that the alimony obligation will definitely terminate at the end of the fixed period would be engaging in speculation on her rehabilitation, and that therefore the matter of continued entitlement to alimony should be reviewed by the court after a certain period.

CHILD SUPPORT

Negotiating child support is now easier and more predictable because the legislature of virtually every jurisdiction, at the encouragement of the federal government, has passed minimum child support guidelines.

Statutory Minimum Child Support Guidelines

Before the recent enactment of state legislation prescribing minimum child support guidelines, many local jurisdictions had informal minimum support guidelines which became the standard in most venues rather than the minimum. It can be anticipated that the statutory minimums also will become more or less the standard, rather than the minimum. This will lend to predictability (which is heaven for a lawyer) but not necessarily to fairness.

For the child support recipient, the important fact is that statutes set forth only guidelines and that these guidelines are for minimums. The actual award of child support needs to be in an amount adequate for the support of the children. The recipient should thus emphasize that the minimum guidelines are only one factor, among several other statutory and case law factors, to be considered.

From the point of view of the child support payor, the emphasis is on the minimum guidelines. He should urge that, barring special circumstances, the minimum guidelines should apply.

The Dual-Income Family and the Guidelines

In this chapter's hypothetical family, we have a dual-income family, which now is the rule rather than the exception, with the husband having the larger income. The shortcoming of virtually every statutory minimum child support guideline is that the formula does not consider a dual-income family. When there is a dual income, the child support payor should argue that child support should be less than the minimum guidelines.

Several dual-income family support guidelines have been published. The most rational approach is contained in an American Bar Association publication, *All About Support*. Some of these dual-income formulas are arbitrary, but under any dual-income formula, the obligation for child support is somewhat less than under the statutory minimum guidelines. The child support obligor should therefore urge either a rather arbitrary reduction from the minimum guidelines, based on the spouse's income, or urge the use of a dual-income family formula.

CONCLUSION

The basis for successful negotiations is preparation, which should take the form of preparing for trial, while hoping and working for settlement. Trial preparation adds leverage to the negotiating process. After the lawyer knows all the facts of the case, learned both from the client and the other side, alternative settlement scenarios should be formulated.

The initial steps to be taken in negotiating the issues of property, alimony and child support are (1) fact gathering; (2) organizing the facts; and (3) evaluation of financial data. The order in which the issues should be resolved is (1) property division; (2) alimony; and (3) child support.

Resolving issues through trial should be the very last resort. Two lawyers who are steeped in the facts of a case should, by creating alternatives, be able to work out settlement configurations that are better than those imposed by a judge, since the court sees a case within the blinders of trial time and rules of evidence.

CHAPTER TEN
Negotiating Child Custody Cases
— James T. Friedman —

The attorney has to undertake a unique burden in negotiating child custody cases. Typically, emotions of both parents and children run so high that client control is difficult if not impossible. Ulterior motives may also fuel the dispute. Because no-fault divorce forecloses courtroom vindication through a grounds trial on issues of marital misconduct, custody litigation is often the emotional substitute. In addition, some spouses will not hesitate to take an arbitrary or aggressive stance on custody or visitation issues to create settlement leverage for property and support issues.

Sometimes the clearly better custodian concedes custody out of concern that a divisive court battle will be more harmful than leaving the child with the wrong parent. A child may choose the wrong parent because that parent brainwashes the child or creates a sense of guilt or parental need that controls the child's preference. If you as the spouse's attorney see that your client's motives and tactics are likely to harm the child, you may be inclined to act contrary to the client's expressed wishes, and ethical problems will result. Deciding to refuse a case or withdraw from one is a matter of conscience and professional judgment, made more difficult by the fact that the client's best interest is not always served by following his or her emotional directives.

The attorney must retain independent judgment, rather than being swept up in a client's extreme anger and emotion. There is no room for blind advocacy in child custody cases. A standard adversarial approach may have to be tempered to avoid harming the child and, perhaps, your own client.

POSITIONING THE CLIENT FOR NEGOTIATION OR TRIAL

To put your client in the best position for negotiation or trial, you first have to understand his priorities and motives. What result does the client really want? If your client's priorities are unrealistic or ill-advised, you may want to work to alter them. You are destined to achieve an unsuccessful result in the client's mind if you do not temper unrealistic client expectations. The lawyer's success in steering a client to reasonable goals is as important as the results ultimately achieved.

Try to discover the priorities and motives of the other spouse and use them to create leverage. Don't concede what the other side wants without a concession in return. Search for alternatives that will appeal to the other side; they may not be aware of alternatives or may want you to be the one to suggest them. The more options and alternatives you bring to a negotiation, the more likely a successful result.

Physical possession of the child and the child's preference of custodian are the keys to winning most custody cases. Accordingly, warn your client not to move out of the marital residence or leave the children in the exclusive care of the other spouse if that can be avoided. Your client can determine whether or not the child has a preference by talking to the child. If there is more than one child involved, usually the one who is more verbal will know the preference of the others. In any case, the client should avoid directly confronting the child with the necessity of choosing between the parents. The child should be assured that he or she is loved by both parents, who will maintain a close relationship with the child notwithstanding the divorce.

CHILD CUSTODY

If the other parent poses a serious threat of physical, psychological, or sexual harm to a child, advise your client to file for court protection immediately. If your state has a domestic violence statute, consider whether invoking it would improve your client's negotiating position, as well as providing protection from actual or threatened abuse. Broad relief is available under these statutes, and the police department can enforce court protective orders.

In interstate disputes, the forum in which you litigate is particularly important because of travel expense, inconvenience, and the tendency of local courts to favor their residents. Accordingly, be conscious of the six months' residence period that creates "home state" jurisdiction under the Uniform Child Custody Jurisdiction Act (UCCJA). In most cases, the home state is the only place where custody cases can be litigated. The UCCJA provides uniform rules for determining child custody jurisdiction among the 50 states. A Federal statute known as the Parental Kidnaping Prevention Act (PKPA) mandates that all states follow the jurisdictional provisions of the UCCJA and makes available services of the Social Security Administration and the Justice Department to locate and return kidnaped children. An attorney who participates in a client's wrongful removal of a child from one state to another may be considered a co-conspirator under criminal child abduction statutes and may be liable for money damages in connection with a tortious interference with parental rights. You should discourage your client from any of these self-help schemes, as they inevitably result in tremendous hardship for the child and the parents.

Don't negotiate or litigate before you have planned a custodial environment for the child. The residence, school, sitter, etc., must be selected, not just contemplated. Hypotheticals rarely prevail over reality. To present an effective case to the court, you should show a specific home, bedroom, etc., and offer testimony from the intended caretakers.

Generally, avoid outside investigations and evaluations unless they will clearly help your case. You don't need experts on every case. They are expensive and can result in substantial delays. Mental health experts can have pet theories or personality problems that lead them to conclusions that may conflict with your theory of the case. The more experts involved, the less control you will have over the presentation of your case. Of course, investigation and evaluation by an expert may be absolutely necessary if there are factual issues which require their expertise. Alleged child abuse and mental health issues are particularly apt for experts. In any event, if the opposition has an expert, you must counter with your own.

TIMING OF THE NEGOTIATION

Good trial preparation is important because it prepares you for negotiation as well as for trial. Thorough preparation also convinces the other side that you are ready and willing to try the case. This creates a certain degree of jeopardy on their part and thereby enhances your credibility and negotiating leverage.

Learn the facts thoroughly. You should complete the investigation of home, school, neighbors, and medical and mental health professionals before you negotiate. You need the facts to exercise your independent, professional judgment. Maybe your client should *not* have sole custody. What is the most likely litigated result? Are there better alternatives that can be negotiated? You must have a reasoned point of view in order to decide. You must be persuasive with your client as well as the other side. You cannot be persuasive without a handle on the facts and a sense of client priorities.

What are your opponent's priorities? Is the other spouse eager to remarry or move out of the state? Is there a school change in the offing or any other event that would be disruptive for the child? The potential for making the other spouse's schedule inconvenient may be a substantial leverage factor, but you must bargain while alternatives still exist. Don't kill the hostages and then negotiate their release.

The timing of any negotiation is crucial. Perhaps financial priorities make the time ripe for a settlement now rather than later. Perhaps your client's bargaining position is at its strongest now because of factors not yet known to the other side such as attorney-client friction, employment or health problems, or pregnancy. If so, make the best deal you can now before your position deteriorates. Busy divorce lawyers tend to service the most anxious clients on the "squeaking wheel" theory. If you discuss priorities at the outset with your clients and make them aware of your case strategy, they will be more likely to squeak at a time when negotiations are appropriate.

ALTERNATIVES TO TRIAL AS FACTORS IN NEGOTIATION

In the 1980's child custody and visitation mediation has developed into a respected problem-resolving process. Mediation is a voluntary procedure whereby individuals submit marital disputes to impartial mediators to assist the participants in achieving a fair settlement. A mediator does not decide the issues like a judge or an arbitrator would. Nor does the mediator provide marriage counseling, as the public often suspects.

While any divorce issue can be mediated, the greatest success has been in the area of custody and visitation. An impartial mediator can be child-oriented and still serve the best interests of both parents without triggering the hostility that a lawyer-adversary often does.

Some jurisdictions require participation in a court-sponsored mediation program before a custody issue can be adjudicated. The programs are as good as the personnel who operate them. Unfortunately, the procedure is sometimes abused by parents who participate in bad faith or for purposes of delay. For the most part, court sponsored mediation has reduced the number of custody trials dramatically.

An effective mediator must recognize and deal with emotional issues and ulterior motives, just as a good lawyer should. A mediator must counter the influence of a dominating parent in the mediation process. Mediation should not be a forum for a bad parent to win custody by domination, and a mediator must be willing to terminate the process and send the matter back for litigation if either party is arbitrary, untruthful, or unconcerned about the child's best interests. A mediator must not force a settlement or allow the dominant or arbitrary spouse to dictate the terms. Mediated settlements must be truly voluntary and based on informed consent if they are to last.

Good mediators cooperate with attorneys, and vice versa. A mediator should not give legal advice and each party needs independent legal counsel as the mediation proceeds. With professional cooperation from the outset, the mediated settlement is much more likely to receive the court approval required to make it effective. Many litigation or negotiation insights and strategies can be gleaned from a failed mediation in which the other spouse's priorities have been revealed. While facts revealed in mediation are supposed to be confidential, that is rarely true in reality.

JOINT CUSTODY

Joint and split custody arrangements are provided for by legislation in most states. They have been the mediator's ultimate settlement ploy for years. Judicial recognition of joint parental rights and responsibilities often will satisfy a litigious parent. Beware, however, of the parent who intends to use joint custody to control or harass the ex-spouse. Joint custody can be a dangerous weapon in the hands of those who remain undivorced psychologically. If undermining parental authority or conflicting discipline practices have been a problem, make sure the physical custodian has ultimate decision-making power.

Spell out the respective rights of both parents and children in the custody or joint parenting agreement. While avoiding language that angers either party, spell out the details of future parent/child contact.

Often people agree to joint custody just to get the case over with. It's probably cheaper for your client and better for the child to meet serious custody problems now rather than later if joint custody is clearly inappropriate.

CHILD CUSTODY

Creative visitation arrangements can be employed to resolve many custody disputes. Most courts are generous with visitation for an interested parent. A properly motivated parent may dispute custody only out of fear that future contact with the child will be unduly restricted. Allaying those fears with liberal, creative visitation arrangements can often give the noncustodial parent better qualitative time with the child than the custodian gets. A parent who arbitrarily seeks to restrict visitation may jeopardize his or her right to custody.

Don't go overboard and victimize the child with bizarre arrangements designed to suit parental whims at the expense of a child's peer activities. The child has a life to lead, and growing up in multiple environments can inhibit the development of community roots and peer relationships. That is not to say that children cannot adapt to differing parenting styles. They clearly can. The parents must recognize, however, that at some point the children will be primarily peer-oriented, and adjustments in the frequency and duration of visits will have to be accommodated.

Try negotiating without using buzz words like "custody" and "visitation." Merely talk and draft in terms of respective parental contact and responsibilities. If you can get the parents thinking in terms of the children's needs, they may become less concerned about winning and losing. Don't be afraid to kick an unreasonable client in the shin, figuratively speaking; the client will appreciate it later. Consider taking your client to task in front of the other side when he or she is clearly wrong on a given point. It is dangerous for client relations, but it enhances your perceived fairness and credibility and may induce concessions out of sympathy for your problems with a difficult client. To avoid instant discharge, it is probably a good idea to alert your client in advance to this negotiating style.

LEVERAGE

Leverage is the application of power or pressure to gain advantage in a negotiation. Whatever you have that the other side wants is a leverage factor. A feeling for leverage factors and their timely, judicious implementation separates negotiation from argument. The art is in recognizing leverage factors that exist at the outset of a case and creating others through careful strategy and case preparation.

Here are some of the most common leverage factors in child custody disputes:

- The child's preference as to residence or custodian. Children will frequently state preferences for house and school rather than for a parent.

- Physical possession of the child pending trial. The parent with sole temporary custody for an extended period generally wins, unless he performs poorly as a custodian.

- The opposing attorney's or client's fear of losing a litigated case. The uncertainty of a litigated outcome creates a sense of jeopardy on the part of both lawyer and client. No one likes to lose.

- Reluctance to litigate because of the effect on the child. Solomon says the parent with this concern ought to have custody.

- Delay caused by litigation. Custody cases can take months or years to finish in court. This can be disruptive to present and future parental plans.

- Time pressures caused by a desire to remarry, move, separate, or take a new job. These are the kinds of future parental plans that are disrupted by litigation. Awareness allows you to use time to your client's advantage.

- The forum of the litigation. There is usually an advantage in litigating in a jurisdiction or before a judge where you are most comfortable. Conversely, unfamiliarity breeds discomfort and creates settlement pressure.

- The promother or profather reputation of the judge or other known tendencies that make the litigated result predictable. Even though justice is supposed to be blind,

CHILD CUSTODY 141

you can bring pressure to bear if the case is set before a judge with tendencies favorable to your client. Don't hesitate to change venue to protect your client from a judge with clearly unfavorable tendencies. Forum shopping may not be noble, but it may be essential, within the rules of the judicial system, if your client is in jeopardy otherwise.

- A party's potential as a bad witness because he or she is emotional, untruthful, or nonverbal. Carefully evaluate each potential witness before electing trial over settlement. Bad witnesses can lose good cases.
- The potential of a party's new spouse or lover as a bad or good witness. That person will be crucial in the child's life and may effect the outcome of a trial more than either parent.
- Health problems of a parent or child that dictate residence in a particular climate, undermine a parent's assertion of fitness, or demand special care of the child. Beware of the situation in which the parent needs the child more than vice versa. That parent will probably lose a custody trial.
- Expert evidence, reports, or evaluations favoring either parent.
- The opinion of the guardian ad litem or attorney for the child—often it will carry more weight with the court than the opinion of an expert retained by one of the spouses.
- Insistence upon psychological evaluations, mediation, and other procedures that may be objected to by the other side because of delay or fear of an unfavorable result.
- Injunctions, domestic violence proceedings, or other temporary motions to inhibit or control the other side or to gain temporary custody of the child. Domestic Violence Act sanctions are very coercive in some jurisdictions and relief is granted rather liberally.
- Pressure to arrive at a joint parenting arrangement. You can induce settlement out of a litigious party by a cleverly

crafted joint parenting agreement that the party can't refuse because it meets his or her priorities. The court may well join you in your efforts.

NEGOTIATING TECHNIQUES

Negotiating techniques are as varied as the styles and personalities of the negotiators. There is no best way; hard or soft or a combination of the two fits certain negotiations and not others. A heavy ("Russian"), threatening style is likely to polarize the parties and exacerbate tensions to the point where communication is impossible. You must convince opposing counsel that your position is reasonable and viable if you expect that position to be recommended to the other spouse. If your facts are inaccurate or your position is arbitrary, you won't be taken seriously. When opposing counsel is alone with his client, he will be your best salesperson if you have been consistently credible.

Make sure you and your client have agreed on a settlement scenario, your factual and legal theory of the case. Both must follow it consistently or you will undermine each other's credibility. If your client contradicts at home what you are saying to opposing counsel, your representation will not be effective.

Demonstrate an ability to control your client. If you can't, convey the inability and try to use the uncontrollable client as a leverage factor—a shared burden, so to speak.

Don't discuss settlement before you have authority from your client. And never discuss settlement unless the other attorney has authority; otherwise you will be sandbagged.

CONCLUSION

While custody negotiations present unique problems for the attorney, credibility and concern for the child's welfare are primary considerations. Thorough trial preparation is a must if negotiations are to be successful, but a fair settlement is better than a good contested victory.

CHAPTER ELEVEN
A Divorce Negotiation Problem: Developing a Strategic Approach

David S. Rosettenstein

It is sometimes said that negotiation is an art, and as such cannot be learned.[1] While the skills of the very best negotiators may derive from inborn talent rather than learning, the fact is that an individual who comes to a negotiation with no knowledge of tactics will be disadvantaged when facing one who has a plan of attack. This chapter uses a mock negotiation exercise to supply a strategic approach to divorce negotiation.

However, this chapter is intended to do more. Apart from offering the negotiator an opportunity to hone such native skills as he or she has, the material should provide a framework for learning about the process of divorce negotiation and enable the participant to better understand his or her role. However, this is not intended to be an exposition of the substantive theory of negotiation. For a theoretical treatment, readers should consult other articles in this book and additional material referred to in the footnotes to this chapter.

Part of the role that an attorney plays in a negotiation is a consequence of his or her position between his client on the one side and the opposing attorney on the other. Though even further removed, the opposing client will also exert a

---

[1] *See generally* H. Edwards & J. White THE LAWYER AS NEGOTIATOR 1–2 (1977).

significant influence on the process.[2] In this regard, a hypothetical problem can use real people to play the role of clients. However, when the problem is presented in a classroom, unless the same person plays the role of client for all attorneys representing one side of the negotiation, these attorneys soon cease to have comparable perspectives. In abstract, this is not really a problem since an attorney has to negotiate with his client's position in mind, whatever that position may be. Nevertheless, the learning process seems to be facilitated if the student can examine not only what he or she did in a given context, but also what everyone else did in essentially the same context.

Accordingly, the problem is drafted so that actors need not play the role of clients. The attorney-negotiators must make do with the confidential written instructions provided, plus the information generally available in the problem. This is not an entirely artificial situation. Divorce practitioners will be all too familiar with the client who is unwilling or unable to assume the responsibility of taking a position on a settlement. In such a context, it becomes the attorney's responsibility to translate into a negotiating posture what are often frustratingly vague instructions. Obviously, it is critical to bear in mind that in real life the settlement must be that of the client.[3]

The problem is meant to be tackled in several phases. Ideally, it should be incorporated into a seminar course and stretched out over several weeks so that considerable attention can be devoted to particular aspects.[4] However, it is possible to compact the entire process so that the preparation, negotiation, and perhaps some written post-negotiation analysis, can

---

[2]C. Liebman, *A Theoretical Basis for Divorce Negotiation* (this volume pp. 1–24) (hereinafter Liebman); P. Sperber, ATTORNEY'S PRACTICE GUIDE TO NEGOTIATION 605–06 (1985) (hereinafter Sperber).

[3]MODEL RULES OF PROFESSIONAL CONDUCT Rule 1.2 (1983); MODEL CODE OF PROFESSIONAL RESPONSIBILITY EC 7–8 (1980); Leatherberry, *Preparing the Client for Successful Negotiation, Mediation and Litigation* 10 (this volume).

[4]A possible schedule can be found *infra* p. 165.

be performed in advance of what would presumably be a fairly lengthy classroom discussion session.

If the negotiation exercise is to be graded, it is suggested that one portion of the grade be assigned for preparation work and written analysis, with another portion to be based on the outcome of the negotiation. One method of determining the grade for the outcome portion of the negotiation is to require that the net financial benefit/detriment of each settlement be reduced to a present value dollar amount using a predetermined formula and discount rate. Even if precision is not demanded in the discounting process, the signatories should reach agreement on what the present value of their agreement is. Student grades will then be based on how well each did relative to the other students who were negotiating on the same side of the dispute.

There may be objections to this grading technique, especially because a portion of the dispute centers around the issue of child custody, which has no monetary value. Thus, it can be argued that the problem invites the use (or more aptly abuse) of the issue of custody of the child in the larger financial and emotional scenario.[5] Practitioners will recognize a problem that is encountered all too frequently. To the extent that the attorney-negotiator is aware of the problem, the lengths to which he or she should go in controlling it is a matter of defining both sound practice and the professional ethics involved.[6] At any rate, whatever one's view of the proprieties of divorce negotiation in general, and the grading scheme in particular, it is desirable to raise the question so that the student negotiator can develop a personal position on the issue.[7]

---

[5]Liebman, *supra* note 2, at 23. Sperber, *supra* note 2, at 621.

[6]*Id.* MODEL CODE OF PROFESSIONAL RESPONSIBILITY EC 7-8 (1980). *See also infra* text accompanying notes 34 and 35.

[7]MODEL CODE OF PROFESSIONAL RESPONSIBILITY EC 7-8 recognizes that an attorney should be in a position to draw a distinction between what is legally permissible and what is morally just. The code suggests that the attorney should be able to identify

THE PROBLEM

Tom and Mary were married eight years ago in Riverton, a town in [select a suitable state]. At the time of the marriage, Mary was 18 and had just graduated from high school. Tom was 22 and had just graduated from college. After the marriage, Mary went to work as a bank teller with a salary of $14,000 a year, and Tom worked as a salesperson in a stereo store and earned $16,000 a year. The couple bought a house using a $10,000 gift from Tom's grandfather. According to Tom, the money was a gift to him by way of an advancement against an inheritance. According to Mary, it was a gift to both of them because the grandfather, she said, wanted them "to buy a house, have children, and continue the family name." The grandfather has since died, and there is no other evidence on this question except for the fact that the grandfather's will made no provision for Tom.

A year or so after the marriage, Mary gave birth to a boy named John, now seven years old. Apart from three months of paid maternity leave, Mary continued to work at the bank. While the couple worked, John initially was in day care and in later years spent the time after school with a babysitter. The couple still found it hard to meet their financial needs, but Tom nevertheless decided that he wanted to become a professional because he was "sick and tired of getting no respect as a salesperson."

Accordingly, Tom enrolled in law school. Mary continued to work in the bank to support the family, and Tom obtained some educational loans and worked part-time and over the summers. During Tom's three years in law school, Mary's gross earnings were $54,000 and Tom's gross earnings were $12,000.

---

possible harsh consequences that might flow from adopting what is otherwise a legally permissible position. In the situation outlined in the text, the harsh consequences may range from a breakdown in the negotiations to further damage to the relationship between the parties and the children. *See also* Liebman, *supra* note 2; Sperber, *supra* note 2.

NEGOTIATION CASE STUDY

Unfortunately, while Tom was in law school the couple drifted apart. Tom became frustrated because Mary showed no interest in what he considered to be intellectually stimulating topics such as the rule against perpetuities. In Mary's view, "law school socialized Tom into the legal profession and out of the human race." The day after he heard that he had passed the state bar examination, Tom filed for divorce. Mary filed a counterclaim. In addition to a divorce, both parties are arguing over custody of John, alimony, child support, and property division, as provided for by state law, and such further ancillary relief as the court deems appropriate.

The following information relating to their financial position is available to both parties:

Matrimonial Home:

The couple own a house held in joint tenancy with a right of survivorship. The equity is $15,000; the mortgage balance is $30,000; the mortgage payments (including taxes and insurance) are $425 per month ($300 is interest); and repairs and maintenance cost $1,000 per year.

Furnishings:

These have a total worth of $10,000. All were purchased during the marriage. There are sufficient duplicates to furnish an apartment minimally. The value of the duplicates is $2,000.

Pensions:

Tom contributed $50 per month to a pension scheme while working as a salesperson. His employer made no additional contribution. However, Tom's interest in the pension never vested. Mary has contributed to a pension scheme at the rate of $50 per month for the last eight years. Her employer has matched this with a further $50 per month. However, Mary's interest in the pension plan generally will not vest unless Mary remains with the bank for a further two years (that is, after 10 years of employment). The pension will not mature until Mary reaches the age of 58—that is in, 32 years. At that time, if contributions continued at their present rate, it is estimated that Mary would become entitled to a pension of $1,500 per month (present dollar value) guaranteed to be paid to his or her estate for 10 years. If Mary dies before the pension matures, and regardless of whether or not it has vested, her estate will be entitled to a lump sum death benefit equal to the total contributions paid by Mary (but not her employer) to the date of her death, plus 6 percent.

Savings:

The couple has a joint savings account of $5,000, which earns $30 per month in interest. The origin of the funds in the account is not clear.

Cars:

The couple own two cars, title to which is in the names of both parties subject to the finance company's lien. The two cars are a Subaru station wagon with an equity value of $3,700, and a Toyota Corolla sedan (two years "younger" than the Subaru) with an equity value of $1,300.

Miscellaneous Liabilities:

Credit Card: The parties are jointly liable on a credit card agreement. The present outstanding balance is $2,500. Payments are $20 per month.

Car Financing: The parties are jointly liable on the notes. The outstanding obligations are: Subaru, 30 monthly payments of $150; Toyota, 40 monthly payments of $200.

NEGOTIATION CASE STUDY

Student Loan: Tom is solely liable on the note. The obligation requires 120 monthly payments of $200.

Employment:

Mary: Gross Salary $19,500 per year F.I.C.A. contributions $1,450. Pension deduction $600.

Tom: Gross salary $26,500 per year F.I.C.A. contributions $2,000.

Employment Prospects:

Mary: Mary is at the top of the salary scale for a bank teller. If she remains a teller, the most she can hope for by way of salary increases in future years is a cost-of-living increase to match inflation. Moreover, she cannot be promoted to a higher position because she lacks a college degree. Additionally, Mary has not seriously considered changing jobs or getting more education in the near future (although she would like to in the long run), because she plans to have custody of John, and banking hours would allow her to be available when he was home from school.

Tom: After passing the bar, Tom obtained employment with the law firm of Wade, Driscoll and Associates, P.C.. Tom's father, Bert Wade, is the senior partner with a controlling interest in the firm. When he took Tom into the firm, his father told Tom that he would be treated "just as any other associate." Thus, Tom's salary of $26,500 is the same as that of any other first-year associate. On this basis, Tom could expect to earn $29,000 (in present-day-dollar terms) in his second year, $33,000 in his third year, $38,000 in his fourth year, and $45,000 in his fifth year. Associates come up for partnership consideration at the end of the fifth year. If the associate fails to make partner, he or she is "out."

If the associate makes partner, earnings are too closely linked to bonuses to be predictable. The only information available is that the actuarial value of a legal education in the state (defined as the average difference between the lifetime earnings of a person with a law degree and the lifetime earnings of a person with only a four-year college degree, with the result discounted to a present value amount) is $102,000. In reality, Bert Wade has high hopes for Tom. The reason is that Mary's father is the Hon. Orvil McCree, generally considered to be the most powerful and influential judge in the state. Judge McCree is reputed to be both aggressively partisan and vindictive. Thus, on Bert Wade's analysis, potential clients are likely to be anxious to employ the services of Wade, Driscoll and Associates because these potential clients will feel that, directly or indirectly, Judge McCree will ensure that theoretically blind justice will look with favor upon those who are clients of the judge's son-in-law's firm.

Supplemental Financial Information:

In using this information, you should treat the child John as just another person. Food costs, per week, per person, are $40. Utilities, per month, per household, are $100. Uninsured medical and dental bills, per year, per person, are $200. The insurance premium would be paid by the adult's respective employers. John could be covered at no additional premium cost to either of the parties.

Transportation expenses, per car, per year (including insurance, but excluding finance payments), are $2,000.

Clothing costs, per person, per year, are $1,000. It would cost $275 a month to rent an efficiency apartment; $325 a month to rent a one-bedroom apartment; and $425 a month to rent a two-bedroom apartment.

Personal expenses, per person, per year, are $1,000.

Assume that for federal income tax purposes, mortgage interest is the only interest payment that a taxpayer can claim by way of an itemized deduction. Assume that the parties are not required to pay any state or local income taxes. Prior to reaching any settlement, both parties live in the matrimonial home and share all expenses equally, except that each party makes his or her own F.I.C.A. payment. Mary contributes 42 percent of the parties' federal tax payment and Tom pays 58 percent. The couple filed a joint federal tax return.

NEITHER ATTORNEY MAY SETTLE THE CASE IF HIS OR HER CLIENT CANNOT AFFORD THE SETTLEMENT.

DEVELOPING AN APPROACH

Introduction

The literature on negotiation is filled with instructions to identify your side's best alternative to a negotiated agreement—now commonly reduced to the acronym BATNA.[8] However, it has been recognized that the feasibility of accurately establishing a BATNA diminishes once one moves away from a simple scenario of, say, a would-be item purchaser who knows that, if the present negotiation falls through, the item can always be obtained from an alternative supplier at a known price.[9] Uncertainty is immediately present once adjudication is the alternative to negotiation. Even if the claim is relatively straightforward, uncertainty associated with the process of litigation—for example, what theory of recovery will be selected by the court, what evidence is available or will be admitted, which witness will be believed—tends to make the identification of a BATNA difficult.

---

[8]R. Fisher & W. Ury, GETTING TO YES 101 *et seq.* (hereinafter Fisher & Ury) (origin of this specific characterization of the proposition that you should try to define what is the best you can hope for if you cannot settle).

[9]Liebman, *supra* note 2, at 14.

The difficulty of establishing a BATNA is pushed to extremes in the context of divorce litigation. Part of the reason is that in virtually every jurisdiction, the law regulating the various aspects of such litigation generally permits the court to exercise a very broad discretion.[10] Accordingly, determining a BATNA in these cases involves predicting how this discretion will be exercised. Moreover, the result that identifying a BATNA requires one to predict is not just a single, simple decision. The facts usually require the court to make what are theoretically a series of independent, discretionary decisions. In reality, because of the court's particular analytical framework, a single, critical decision often triggers an entire package of decisions. For example, a decision that X is to get custody of a child may trigger the conclusion that X must also (at least) have occupancy of the former matrimonial home. In turn, this may trigger a variety of possible "axiomatic" support orders. And so on.

Against a backdrop of such complex discretionary decision-making, a negotiated settlement has a distinct advantage over litigation. In particular it helps minimize the risk of being the recipient of an unwanted discretionary package.[11] Nevertheless, it is important for divorce negotiators to appreciate that such packages exist, albeit only in general terms. For one thing, the package may be along the lines of what the client desires. If the negotiator's BATNA analysis suggests that the court is likely to make the basic triggering decision, the thrust of the negotiation often need only be directed at fine-tuning the package—assuming, of course, that the other side has reached the same conclusion. If not, persuading the other side to reach the same conclusion may be a significant component of the negotiation. Conversely, the thrust of at least one side's concerns in the negotiation may be to persuade the other side through reasoned discussion that on the basis of the facts or law applicable to the case, reliance on a particular package

---

[10]Mnookin & Kornhauser, *Bargaining in the Shadow of the Law: The Case of Divorce*, 88 YALE L.J. 950, 969–71, 977–80 (1979) (hereinafter Mnookin).

[11]*Id.* at 974.

NEGOTIATION CASE STUDY

approach is inappropriate. Additionally, or alternatively, an effort may be made through the use of one or more tactical devices,[12] not necessarily stopping short of threats, to induce the other side not to rely on any anticipated standard approach by the court.

Because so much of the outcome of divorce litigation hinges on how discretionary authority is exercised locally, if the problem negotiation is conducted in a seminar or similar course it is recommended that the instructor determine in advance which currently sitting judge will supposedly hear the case. Ideally, at the earliest possible stage of preparation, students should spend a day in that judge's court. In addition, and at the very least, it is desirable that transcripts be obtained of a number of divorce trials presided over by that judge,[13] so that students can analyze them in order to develop a sense (in the same way that an experienced practitioner would) of how that court tends to exercise its discretion.

Know the Law

It may seem trite to say that the negotiator should know the law regulating the dispute since, as indicated above,[14] legal research may yield little more than a series of broad discretionary principles. Nevertheless, knowledge of the legal minutiae, to the extent that they exist, will enable the negotiator to confirm as legitimate an opponent's purported reliance on objective criteria,[15] or threat,[16] where these are supposedly

---

[12]Skoloff, *The Art and Craft of Successful Negotiation* (this volume pp. 37–45); Sperber, *supra* note 2, at 617–28. More generally, *see* Fisher & Ury, *supra* note 8; H. Raiffa, THE ART AND SCIENCE OF NEGOTIATION (1982); T. Schelling, THE STRATEGY OF CONFLICT (1960).

[13]Former students who have participated in the seminar make excellent "scouts" for suitable cases, particularly if they are clerking in local courts.

[14]*See supra* text accompanying note 10.

[15]Fisher & Ury, *supra* note 8, at 88 *et seq.*

[16]Sperber *supra* note 2, at 626. *But see* Fisher & Ury, *supra* note 8, at 142–43.

based on the law. Thus, to illustrate, beyond the broad general principles, the negotiator should be aware that while the jurisdiction's laws will not permit the distribution of property acquired by one party after the marriage ceased to be viable, this property will be available for distribution if it was acquired with assets that could have been distributed.[17] Or the negotiator should know that the jurisdiction will permit a corporate veil to be pierced in order to establish that it is no more than an alter ego of a party, so that the assets and income of the corporation can be attributed to that party in the context of matrimonial litigation.[18]

Another valuable function that knowledge of the law can perform is to help identify which subjects *must* as distinct from *may* be agreed upon. For example, if the law does not permit a court to order the equitable distribution of an inheritance[19] or portions of a military pension,[20] the beneficiary who seeks to retain the relevant assets need not negotiate over them. On the other hand, the fact that these assets are not subject to control by the divorce court may provide the negotiator with a valuable bargaining chip and a means of inventing a settlement option.[21]

Much negotiation literature deals with the problem of "distributive" bargaining—negotiating in the context of a zero-sum game where one person's gain is another's loss, and where the outcome supposedly depends on the relative bargaining power of the parties.[22] The assumption of many attorneys seems to be that divorce negotiation falls into this

---

[17]Hunt v. Hunt, 698 P.2d 1168 (Alaska 1985).

[18]Krajcovic v. Krajcovic, 693 S.W.2d 884 (Mo. Ct. App. 1985).

[19]N.J. STAT. ANN. sec. 2A:34–23 (West 1983).

[20]UNIF. SERVICES FROMER SPOUSES' PROTECTION ACT, 10 U.S.C. 1450 (f) (3) (1982).

[21]*See* Fisher & Ury, *supra* note 8, at 58 *et seq.*; Liebman, *supra* note 2, at 22–23.

[22]White, *The Pros and Cons of "Getting to Yes"*, 34 J. LEGAL EDUC. 115, 115 (1984); Schelling, *supra* note 12, at 21. *Contra*, Fisher & Ury, *supra* note 8, at 61. For one view of what constitutes negotiating power see Fisher, *Negotiating Power*, 27 AM. BEHAV. SCI. 149 (1983).

category.[23] However, at least from the point of view that focuses on what is in a party's interests[24] with certain fact patterns the process can be "integrative," that is, produce a result in which the parties get what each wants at a perceived cost to neither. This may be especially true when an interest revolves around the issue, important but impossible to quantify, of a child's well-being.[25]

Regardless of whether divorce negotiation normally is "distributive" in character, knowledge of the tax law consequences of possible settlements may lift the negotiation out of the zero-sum arena into a situation of relative benefit to both parties. A well-negotiated settlement obviously should deal with such matters as the exchange of tax information and records. Additionally, the creative use of the distinction between alimony and property division orders, the availability of exemptions, child care credits, head-of-household filing status, and so on, may well mean that in a cooperative negotiation it will be possible to increase the funds available for distribution between the parties. Moreover, even in a less cooperative environment, a knowledge of the applicable tax law is essential—if for no other purpose than minimizing one's client's tax burden.

As a component of a seminar course, students may be required to compile a summary of the applicable principles of law.

Know the Facts

It also seems obvious that a negotiator must know the facts of the case. Yet practically, this may present problems in divorce cases because the parties may not possess equal knowledge of the relevant facts, particularly of the financial facts. Clearly this is a situation that depositions and interrogatories are intended to remedy.

---

[23]Sperber, *supra* note 2, at 617.
[24]Fisher & Ury, *supra* note 8, at 41 *et seq.*
[25]Mnookin, *supra* note 10, at 964.

The facts that a negotiator should know go beyond knowledge of the monthly payments. In divorce cases many apparently simple facts turn out to be rather complex, and not simply materially but emotionally or psychologically. A simple negotiating stance might be, "I want the car because it is a valuable asset." If the other party wants the car as a means of transport, a settlement is often readily effected through an appropriate economic exchange, at least when there are adequate financial resources. However, if the proposition is, "I want the car because I am going to have custody of Johnny and I need the car to get him to school," at the very least we have additional complexity (still at a material level), since the ownership of the car is tied to the question of custody, the issue of transport to school, or both. If the questions of custody and the identity of the person doing the transporting to and from school are governed by the state of Johnny's emotional well-being, negotiating the ownership of the car may become very difficult indeed. In any event it is critical for the negotiator to identify the extent to which negotiation claims are factually linked. This is really a key to "interest"-oriented negotiation.[26]

Finally, it is important to see the facts not just as isolated entities but as an integrated whole. For example, even though particular proposals may be acceptable to the other side, the cumulative impact of all the proposals may be too much to accept. Clearly this would be a concern if this is a negotiation focusing on the parties' "interests."[27] But even when the agreement is more or less imposed on the other side, the proponent of the terms would be advised to look to the total factual impact of those terms. At best it is debatable whether a divorce agreement will be complied with if its provisions are cumulatively unreasonable—particularly its financial provisions.[28]

A useful exercise aimed at developing an understanding of the interdependency of the components of the financial and factual arrangements is to require seminar students to prepare

---

[26]Fisher & Ury, *supra* note 8, at 41 *et seq.*
[27]*Id.*
[28]Liebman, *supra* note 2, at 21.

financial affidavits or statements in the form obligatory under local practice rules. Two such statements should be required from each side. The first statement should be based on the party's position prior to entering the agreement, with the relevant details extracted from the financial information supplied with the problem. This statement would be the analog of the one that most jurisdictions require the parties to provide the court at the time of the dissolution hearing. The second statement should reflect the future situation, when the parties will be living subject to the agreement reached. One of the purposes of this second statement is to ensure that the parties do not settle on a basis that one or the other of them cannot afford. That would violate a basic principle regulating the negotiation, and more importantly, would set up a situation that in real life would provide an open invitation to noncompliance.

Negotiating Policy and Ethics

The act of negotiation, in whatever context, raises ethical dilemmas for an attorney. Although it is generally accepted that an attorney-negotiator is required to abide by standards of honesty and fair dealing,[29] the actual application of these principles presents considerable difficulty.[30] Moreover, whatever the ethical perimeters for an attorney-negotiator in general, there are particular difficulties when the negotiation centers around marriage dissolution. It is not just fortuitous that Fisher resorts to a divorce hypothetical when outlining a quest for a better way to negotiate generally. In particular, he asks, if a husband and wife were to approach an expert for a way to negotiate a wise and fair divorce settlement that would best enable them to deal with future problems while minimizing costs in terms of resources and stress, would they receive different advice depending upon whether the approach was made jointly or separately?[31]

---

[29]Skoloff, *supra* note 12, at 13. MODEL RULES OF PROFESSIONAL CONDUCT Rule 4.1 (1983).

[30]White, *Machiavelli and the Bar: Ethical Limitations on Lying in Negotiation*, 1980 A.B.F. RES. J. 926 (hereinafter White).

While an attorney is committed to vigorously representing his or her client's interests, the unique character of matrimonial litigation requires particular care by the attorney-negotiator, both as a matter of ethics and sound negotiation practice, in determining where that client's interests really lie. Approaches to negotiation that could be considered ethical in a strictly technical light might nevertheless be perceived as unprofessional,[32] or at very least disadvantageous to the client, if the price of a limited negotiation victory is incessant warfare for as long as the settlement is operative.[33] The need for ethical and professional care is heightened because of the inordinately close proximity of the parties both before and after the negotiation. White points out[34] that one of the difficulties with attempting to establish such ethical standards is that the negotiations are usually conducted in private, so that identifying and proving a lack of ethicality is difficult. The proximity of the parties in a divorce negotiation means that the risk of discovery is greater. But more important, the risk of a perceived lack of ethicality is greater.[35]

Many divorce negotiations require the resolution of issues relating to custody and support of children. Some jurisdictions automatically require that a guardian *ad litem* or attorney be appointed to protect the interests of a child in these cases.[36] However, in many instances individual representation for the

---

[31] Fisher, *Comment*, 34 J. LEGAL EDUC. 120, 120 (1984).

[32] For one view of how professionalism requires a moral perspective *see* Fried, *The Lawyer as Friend: The Moral Foundation of the Lawyer-Client Relationship*, 85 YALE L.J. 1060 (1976) (hereinafter Fried).

[33] Liebman, *supra* note 2, at 26.

[34] White, *supra* note 30, at 926.

[35] The exploitation by lawyers of matters of intimacy and confidences between the parties is likely to be readily perceived as unethical—though the exact point at which the lawyer's conduct will be considered as, say, the needless infliction of harm (*see* MODEL CODE OF PROFESSIONAL RESPONSIBILITY EC 7-8 (1980)) will be hard to identify. Accordingly, it might be more appropriate to consider the lawyer's conduct as immoral rather than unethical. On the issue of immoral means, see Fried, *supra* note 32, at 1082.

[36] WIS. STAT. ANN. sec. 767.045 (West 1981).

child will be required only if it appears unlikely that the issues can be resolved short of the courthouse door.[37] In consequence, there is a real risk that a child will be unrepresented when a settlement is negotiated. Technically, from the negotiating attorney's point of view, the child is neither client nor opposition. Does this mean that the attorney can exploit the child or disadvantage the child to advance his or her own client's interests and still be considered ethical and professional?

Whatever the precise technical posture taken by professional standards bodies in the various jurisdictions, it is certain that there will be significant gray areas in the ethical and professional conduct of divorce negotiations. Inevitably the attorney-negotiator will have to decide subjectively on the standards for these gray areas.

In a seminar course, students can be required to research and compile a summary of the jurisdiction's ethical and professional standards for divorce negotiation as part of their research into the applicable law.[38] Then, in the course of preparing for the negotiation, students should formulate their own ethical position in relation to the actual facts of the case.[39]

Preparing for the Negotiation

One of the easiest techniques to use in preparing for the negotiation is to develop an extensive checklist of all items for which relief is sought. This would cover not only physical points—ranging, for example, from the matrimonial home, through insurance payments, to an exchange of tax documents—but also, when relevant, to custody, visitation, school information, and the like. The checklist may be developed in the following way:

(a) List all the matters you would like to have covered by the settlement. With respect to *each matter*:

---

[37]Yontef v. Yontef, 185 Conn. 275, 284, 440. A.2d 899, 904 (1981).
[38]*See supra* p. 153.
[39]*See infra* p. 160.

(i) What is your most-desired settlement position?

(ii) Why is this the most-desired settlement position? In answering this and similar questions below, try to decide whether this decision is based on the operative law, on the relevant facts, on tactical considerations, or on a combination of these factors. Knowing the reason why a particular position was adopted will help indicate areas where flexibility might be possible or desirable, depending on how the negotiation progresses.

(iii) What is the minimum settlement position that would be acceptable to you?

(iv) Why is this your minimum settlement position?

(v) What do you anticipate will be the other side's most-desired settlement position?

(vi) Why do you anticipate this will be their most-desired settlement position?

(vii) What do you anticipate will be the other side's minimum settlement position?

(viii) Why do you suppose this will be their minimum settlement position?

(ix) Are there any matters you will settle in the manner just decided only if other matters are settled in a particular way? If so, how do you propose that these matters be settled if you cannot get those others settled the way you want?

(x) Does your analysis of the various bargaining positions adequately take into account local court practices, particularly practices relating to the court's discretionary authority? Would any of your intended settlement positions be questioned and possibly modified by a court asked to approve the agreement?

(b) Based on the above analysis, are there any points on

NEGOTIATION CASE STUDY 161

which you foresee ready agreement? If there are such matters, at what stage of the negotiation do you think that they should be settled? Why?

(c) Does the above analysis suggest that there are any matters on which reasoned integrative bargaining[40] will produce a settlement, at least after significant effort? Why?

(d) If there are any matters that you anticipate will be left unsettled under (b) and (c) above, what techniques of distributive bargaining[41] might produce a settlement? Even if the chosen techniques are normally capable of producing a settlement on these matters, will the employment of such techniques be likely to have any unwanted side effects—for example, by endangering possible agreement on other matters or by endangering the viability of any future relationship the parties might need or desire to have?[42] Is the risk of these side effects nevertheless justified? Do you consider that the other side will use any of these techniques, regardless of whether you consider their use justified? If so, how do you plan to respond?

(e) Do you consider that the cumulative effect of a settlement with terms in the range you propose will produce an agreement with which the other side is likely to comply?[43] If the answer to this question is no, are there any matters you should concede even if this means going below your minimum position?

(f) Is there any component of the proposed settlement, a matter either of substance or process, which is of doubtful ethicality or professionalism?[44] If so, how do you propose to resolve these doubts?

---

[40] *See supra* the text accompanying notes 22–25.
[41] *Id.*
[42] *See supra* the text accompanying notes 31–33.
[43] *See supra* the text accompanying notes 27–28.
[44] *See supra* p. 159.

(g) Do you know anything about the character or personality of the attorneys or clients that might affect your approach and the issues of when and where the negotiation should be conducted?[45]

As part of a seminar course, students would be required to prepare and submit a written analysis along the above lines before commencing negotiation.

Negotiate

Seminar students are given a deadline by which they must have submitted a written settlement agreement or be deemed to have failed to settle. Beyond that, students receive the opportunity of deciding where and when to negotiate and how much time to devote to the negotiation.

Students must submit a written settlement agreement signed by both parties, although the instructor may require the agreement in outline form only. Alternatively the instructor may use this negotiation as an opportunity for the students to master the skills of drafting a settlement instrument and accordingly require the submission of a detailed and comprehensive agreement.

The instructor should determine whether the students will be required to submit an agreed-upon present value of the settlement.[46]

Post-Negotiation Analysis

The conclusion of the negotiation is not the end of the learning process. Clearly any negotiator, however skilled, will benefit from a retrospective appraisal of the negotiation process and its results. In the context of a seminar, students could be required to submit a written analysis along these lines:

---

[45] For a psychologist's insights, *see* K. Kresel, THE PROCESS OF DIVORCE 30–64, 168, 177 (1985).

[46] *See supra* section A, paragraph preceding that containing note 5.

(a) Was there any item that the settlement was originally supposed to cover but was not included in the final agreement? Omission by oversight is obviously unacceptable and can be readily avoided by preparing a detailed checklist in advance. More important are items that were deliberately not dealt with directly. To what extent was an item omitted because the final structure of the settlement made it unnecessary to deal with the item? Does that indicate the final form is more efficient than what was originally contemplated? If the matter was deliberately left unresolved for reasons other than the form of the settlement, why? Was this result anticipated as a possibility? Were there indications that the other side wanted the omitted issue resolved, and if so, why didn't the other side pursue it? Is the answer to any of these questions generally relevant or applicable to other divorce negotiations?

(b) With respect to each item covered in the settlement, to what extent did the agreed-upon result differ from the best possible and minimum acceptable results originally contemplated for either side? In each case, why did this difference occur? Could a different result have been achieved if either side had used a different approach? To what extent does this go beyond simply using a different numerical starting point? If the result was below an anticipated minimum or beyond an anticipated maximum, was this due to an initial error in fixing the maximum or minimum, or was it due to what occurred in the bargaining process itself? If it was due to an initial error, why did this error occur? Was it a tactical error, due to inadequate legal or factual preparation, or can it be attributed to some other cause? If the unforeseen result was due to what occurred in the bargaining process itself, was this a consequence of a calculated move by the other side? Of a failure to respond adequately to the other side? Was it a consequence of an appropriate response? In any event, can principles of general applicability be gleaned from the result or the process through which it occurred?

(c) What do you think of the negotiating style *and* technique of the negotiator on the other side? Do you consider that style or technique effective? Why? To the extent you believe that the negotiator's style or technique contained positive elements, would you think about adopting them for yourself? Explain why you reach the conclusion that you do. Do you think that the negotiator on the other side would rate you as an effective negotiator? Why? Were there any elements of style or technique either on your part or on the part of the other negotiator that you consider particularly appropriate or inappropriate in a divorce negotiation setting? Explain your thinking on this point. Regardless of their appropriateness, do you consider that these elements of style or technique were particularly effective? Explain your reasoning. Do you think that their effectiveness was due to the fact that they were used in a divorce negotiation, or do you think they would be effective in most negotiations? Do your answers to any of the above questions depend on whether one or both clients were physically present at the negotiation?

(d) To what extent was your approach to the negotiation or the ultimate settlement influenced by your perception of how the "assigned" trial judge would have dealt with the case if it had gone to trial?[47] Do you think that the other side was influenced by the same factors?

(e) To what extent were the form of the settlement and the terms that you agreed to consequences of your own subjective preferences? Would the situation have been different if you'd had an actual client from whom to take instructions?

---

[47]*See supra* the text accompanying note 13.

A Possible Timetable for Use In a Seminar Course

First Week:

During this meeting, the problem should be distributed along with any supplementary reading lists. Grading principles should be outlined, including penalties for late delivery of written work as well as for failure to ensure that issues of alimony, child support, property division, and custody are adequately resolved. If it is intended to visit the court of the judge who notionally will hear the case if it is not settled, schedule the visit. Establish a general timetable for the course. At this stage, the students should *not* be assigned to a particular side of the negotiation, nor should confidential instructions be distributed. A procedure should be established for dealing with difficulties that may occur regarding the problem or the negotiation process in general.

Second and Third Week:

Students should submit a written summary of the applicable legal and ethical principles governing the negotiation. The relevant principles can be discussed in class. Students should now be assigned to represent either the husband or wife and should receive a copy of the relevant confidential instructions.

Fourth Week:

Students should study and discuss the transcripts of trials presided over by the "assigned" judge. If the judge's court is to be visited, the visit should precede any discussion.

Fifth, Sixth and Seventh Weeks:

Students should submit a written financial statement in the form required by local rules, reflecting the client's position as it would be if the case went to trial unsettled. Students should also submit a written divorce strategy checklist dealing with the issues outlined on pages 159–161.

Eight and Ninth Weeks:

Negotiation in progress.

10th Week:

Students should submit a written settlement agreement, either in outline or detailed form (depending upon what the course calls for), as well as a post-settlement financial statement.

11th, 12th, and 13th Weeks:

Students should submit a detailed written post-negotiation analysis dealing with the topics raised on pages 162–164. A substantial amount of time should be made available for classroom discussion of these matters and any others arising from the negotiation.

ANNEXURE A
CONFIDENTIAL INSTRUCTIONS TO TOM'S ATTORNEY

Part of the reason for the breakdown of the marriage is that Tom has become romantically involved with Kate, a fellow law student. However, Tom has no wish to marry or live with Kate after his divorce. As far as Tom is aware, Mary does not know of his relationship with Kate, but he cannot be absolutely certain of this. Tom is concerned that Mary not find out about Kate. He thinks this is quite possible if the matter is not settled before trial. Tom is also concerned that his affair should not come to the attention of Judge McCree—

especially if it becomes public knowledge in the course of a trial. Tom's father, Bert Wade, is aware of the affair and it is his view, shared by Tom, that if Judge McCree, with his reputed vindictiveness, should hear of the affair, the odds might be stacked against any Wade, Driscoll client who had to go to trial in the future. Bert's position is that even if this isn't true, it would be perceived as true by members of the public looking for an attorney. Accordingly, Bert has told Tom that if the case goes to trial, Tom will be summarily dismissed from Wade, Driscoll. Indeed, in Tom's view, if the affair should become public knowledge, he would probably be unemployable as an attorney anywhere in the state. Thus, you are instructed to do your utmost to prevent the affair with Kate from coming to the judge's attention. You must not confirm the existence of the affair to Mary's attorney, and you must do everything possible to avoid a contested trial.

On the question of custody, Tom wants you to be seen as vigorously trying to obtain sole custody of John. Tom wants to be sure that if an analysis is made after the divorce, no one will ever be able to convince John that his father did not put up a fight for sole custody. In fact, Tom would prefer joint custody, and, if pushed, would admit to being willing not to have custody at all, provided that he could have flexible and extensive visitation rights, including the right to have John stay overnight and for extended periods during vacation time. But Tom keeps returning to the point that you must be seen as putting up a very strong fight for sole custody. Thus, you are instructed to concede the question of sole custody *only as a last resort*.

Tom's financial instructions are relatively simple. He wants to pay the least possible and get the most possible.

Tom is adamant that you should do everything you can to avoid his having to pay alimony, because "she will always be coming back for more." At very worst, he would accept having to pay a "small" amount of alimony provided he could be assured that it was not modifiable and would only be payable for a fixed, "short" period.

Tom would like to keep the house. At any rate, he feels he is entitled to $10,000 of the equity, representing his grandfather's gift and half of any equity beyond that.

Tom is prepared to be "reasonable" on the issue of child support, if it should come to that, but his position is that Mary should be responsible for a fair share.

Finally, Tom would like one of the cars, but he doesn't care which one.

ANNEXURE B
CONFIDENTIAL INSTRUCTIONS TO
MARY'S ATTORNEY

Mary has a number of major concerns.

First, Mary's grandfather, Willard McCree, John's great-grandfather, established a trust now worth several million dollars. The trust capital is to be distributed to any of Willard's great-grandchildren on their 18th birthday, provided that these grandchildren have been raised "in the manner and tradition of the McCrees." Apart from John, there is only one other great gandchild, Miles, the son of Mary's sister. Mary and her sister have not spoken for years. Their animosity is so great that Mary knows that given the slightest opportunity, her sister will do anything she can to frustrate John's claim to the trust capital. Mary is concerned, in view of the impending divorce, that if Tom gets custody—even joint custody—of John, Mary's sister will argue that John was not raised "in the manner and tradition of the McCrees." Accordingly, you are instructed to do everything possible to obtain sole custody for Mary. In fact, you may not settle unless you can get sole custody.

Mary is furious that Tom wants to leave her just when the money is starting to come in, after what she sees as all her hard work. Thus Mary's instructions on finances are graphic and simple: "Take him for every cent you can get." Within this framework, Mary is prepared to leave it to you to get the best possible deal. However, she does want to continue to live in the house.

Mary tells you that since the breakdown of the marriage she has become involved with another man, and she thinks this relationship has the possibility of maturing into something permanent. She would like you to bear this in mind in structuring any settlement.

Finally, Mary tells you that for what it is worth, some time before the couple acknowledged their marriage had broken down, some of her friends thought they saw Tom with his arm around another woman. However, it was some distance away, and the friends were not absolutely sure it was Tom.

Index

A

Adversarial approach
  disempowering clients, 20
  divorce disputes posing special dangers for, 16–19
  generally, 5
  missed opportunities for options, 21
  prolonging emotional tension, 20
  risks of, 19–21
  unworkable final agreement, 21
Alimony
  budgets, preparation in accordance with lifestyle, 129
  custodian of children, effect of alimony, 128
  distribution of property effecting, 115–16
  income-producing property, 127–28
  obligation to seek employment, 130–31
  rehabilitative alimony, 130–31
  spouse's employment income ability, 128
  tax consequence, 128–29
  Uniform Marriage and Divorce Act, 127
Antenuptial agreements. *See* Prenuptial agreements
Attorney's fees, 34

C

Characteristics of divorce disputes, 16–19
Child custody
  custodial plans, need for specific plans, 135–36
  difficulties involving, 133–34
  distribution of property effecting, 115–16
  experts, use of, 135–36
  guardian ad litem, 158–59
  home state jurisdiction, 135
  interstate disputes, 135
  joint custody, 138
  kidnaping of child by parent, 135
  leverage, 134, 136, 139–42
  mediation, 137–38
  motives, understanding client's, 134
  negotiating techniques, 142
  physical possession of child, importance of, 134
  preference of child, importance of, 134
  priorities, understanding client's, 134
  timing of negotiations, 136–37
Child support
  dual-income family, 132
  guardian ad litem, 158–59
  minimum support statutes, 131
Client preparation
  active listening, 26–29
  confidence and trust, gaining client's, 26
  interviewing of, 25
  lawyer's fees, 34
  lawyer's judgmental attitude, 31
  presence at negotiations, 40–41, 44
  recognition of client's feelings, 29–30
  reorientating client's emotions, 32–33
  therapy referral, 33–34
  working agreement of, 31–32
Closely held corporation
  valuation of interest for division of property, 124

INDEX

Conferences
  four-way conferences, 48–60
    emotional stage of client, 50
    how many, 52
    inappropriateness of, 49
    interests, focusing on, 58
    options, creating, 59–60
    principled negotiations style, 53–60
    timing of conference, 49–50
  pretrial order conference, 73–79
  principled negotiations style, 53–60

D

Deadlocks, 44
Distribution of property
  alimony and support
    generally affecting, 115–16
    in lieu of, 116
  closely held corporation interest, 124–25
  equitable distribution, 114
  household goods, 116–17
  income producing assets, 117
  individual retirement accounts, 126
  justification of position based on law, 115
  pension plan assets, 122–24
  percentage determination, 114
  professional practice, 125–26
  residence
    delayed sale, factors effecting distribution, 118
    dividing sale proceeds, 118–22
    immediate sale, 119–22
    possession after divorce, factors concerning, 118
  royalties, 125–26
  tax consequences, 115
  tax shelters, 126–27
Dual-income family
  child support, 132

E

Effective negotiations
 principled negotiation, 13–16
 William Study, 13–16
Equitable distributions. *See* Distribution of property
Ethics
 authority, 45
 errors and omissions, 45
 guardian ad litem for children, 158–59
 lying and manipulation, 45
 negotiator's ethics, 157–59
 threats, 43
Experts, use of, 135–36

F

Fairness
 importance of, 113
 prenuptial agreements, 65–66
Financial settlements
 alimony. *See* Alimony
 child support. *See* Child support
 property distribution. *See* Distribution of property
Fisher and Ury Rules. *See* Principled negotiations

G

Gerald Williams, 13–16, 55
Getting to Yes. See Principled negotiations
Guardian ad litem, 158–59

H

Hostility junkies, 78

INDEX

I

Individual retirement accounts, 126

J

Judges
  discretion of court affecting viable alternatives, 152
  guidance from, 77
  idiosyncrasies of judge explained to client, 83–87
  pretrial conference, 73–79, 81
  recommendations by, 76
  role of, 73, 83–87

K

Kidnaping of child, 135

L

Leverage
  child custody, 134, 136, 139–142
  generally, 111

M

Mediation
  advice, prohibition against, 90
  alternatives, 90–93
  balance of power between parties, 100–101
  child custody, 137–38
  client's consul, role of, 108
  confidentiality of, 90
  conflict resolution models, types of, 104–05
  formal commitment, 94

Mediation *(continued)*
  hypothetical options, 105
  inappropriateness of, 93
  initial session, 94–95
  judicial scrutiny of agreement, 98–99
  later session, 107–09
  options, 90–93
  principled negotiations, 102–04
  public policy considerations, 98–99
  scope of, 90
Meetings. *See* Conferences

N

Negotiations
  adversarial approach. *See* Adversarial approach
  atmosphere of meeting, 42, 74
  behavior, aggressive or passive, 42
  case study, 143–169
  checklist for, 159–62
  client's emotional appearance during, 38–40, 44, 50
  client's goals, 37–38, 58–59
  client's presence, 40–41
  complete disclosure, 38
  cooperative approach, 53–56
  deadlocks, 44
  delay, effective, 72
  development of, 39
  effective communication, 39
  ethics. *See* Ethics
  knowlege of facts, mastering, 155–57
  knowledge of law, importance of, 153–54
  leverage
    child custody, 134, 136, 139–42
    generally, 111
  meeting location 40, 51
  offers, 42–43, 59
  prenuptial agreements. *See* Prenuptial agreements

INDEX 177

Negotiations *(continued)*
pretrial conferences, 73–79
principled negotiations. *See* Principled negotiations
role model, negotiator as, 21–24, 47
style, 53
threats, 43
timing of, 41–42, 49, 82

P

Pension plan assets
if-and-when standard, 123–24
part of marital estate, 122
qualified domestic relations orders, 123–24
trading off value when only one spouse has plan, 124
valuation, 122–23
Prenuptial agreements
alternative agreements, 65–66
considerations for, 62–63
full disclosure, 64
guaranteed income, 65
life insurance, 65
provisions understood, 64
right to inherit, 65
validity of, 63
voluntarily entered into, 64
waiver of support, 66–70
Principled negotiations
best-alternative-to-negotiated-agreement approach, 11–13, 52–54, 151–52
dynamics of four-way conference, 56–57
facing opponents with stronger positions, 11–13
focusing on interests, 9–10, 58
generally, 6–7
generating options, 10, 59
mediation, 102–04
results based on objective standards, 11
separating people from problem, 8–9

Professional practice
  distribution of property, 125–26
Property distributions. *See* Distribution of property

R

Realistic settlements
  futile cases, 77–79
  role of court, 73
Residence
  delayed sale, factors effecting distribution, 118
  dividing sale proceeds, 118–22
  immediate sale, 119–22
  possession after divorce, factors concerning, 118
Role model, negotiator as, 21–24, 47
Royalties, 125–26

S

Settlement, pretrial, 72–73
Strategies
  aggressiveness as a tool, 42
  development of, 39
  ethics. *See* Ethics
  gamesmanship, 42–43
  leverage. *See* Leverage
  threat of litigation, 43
  timing of negotiations
    child custody negotiations, 136–37
    conference, 49, 82
    emotional stage of client, 50
Styles of negotiations
  adversarial approach. *See* Adversarial approach
  "effective cooperative" negotiation, 13–16
  principled negotiations. *See* Principled negotiations
  Williams study, 13–16

T

Tax considerations
  alimony, 128–29
  distribution of property, 115
Tax shelters, 126–27
Therapy, referral of clients, 33–34
Threat of litigation, 44
Timing of negotiations
  child custody negotiations, 136–37
  conference, 49, 82
  emotional stage of client, 50

U

Uniform Marriage and Divorce Act. *See* alimony, 127

Z

Zero-sum game. *See* Adversarial approach